# Casebook in College Library Administration

by
ALICE GERTZOG

The Scarecrow Press, Inc.
Metuchen, N.J., & London
1992

British Library Cataloguing-in-Publication data available

Library of Congress Cataloging-in-Publication Data

Gertzog, Alice.
    Casebook in college library administration / by Alice Gertzog.
       p. cm.
    Includes index.
    ISBN 0-8108-2554-6 (acid-free paper)
      1. Libraries, University and college--Administration--Case
studies. I. Title.
    Z675.U5G47 1992
    027.7--dc20                                    92-7358

*For Rachel, Karen, Josh and Ben*

# CONTENTS

# INTRODUCTION

This casebook is designed for use in a course dealing with academic libraries and in management courses, particularly those that include a segment devoted to academic libraries. The cases describe problems which every college librarian will encounter in one form or another. Each has policy, political, practical and procedural implications and should be considered from those perspectives. Questions for consideration are offered, either explicitly or implicitly in the thoughts of the protagonists, at the conclusion of each case to help stimulate discussion, but they have been kept to a minimum to encourage readers to identify for themselves what they believe to be the important issues.

One potential drawback to the case study method is that the cases, characterized by difficult, consequential and often painful choices, sometimes elicit unsystematic or highly emotional responses. All of the cases in this book should be investigated in light of precedent and against the background of information provided in professional literature. Most of the subjects are treated in *Lyle's Administration of the College Library*, academic library or other library management books. Suggested reading lists accompanying the cases will lead readers to sources of information that treat issues not addressed directly in the texts. As an example, Case Six requires students to consult at least three different bodies of library literature: works discussing buildings, studies of staffing, and explorations of library use patterns. Analysis of Case One will profit from a well-developed grasp of the relationship between curriculum and library holdings, as well as from a knowledge about the current status of Women's Studies programs in undergraduate curricula. Case Five may be best approached as a written assignment, with class discussion centering on alternate routes students have taken to solve the problem. Responses to this case, too, will be enriched by reference to the extensive literature about how college libraries organize themselves.

There are no right or wrong answers to the problems. The cases present sets of circumstances that evoke conflict, and readers are asked only to select the best responses from among imperfect options. The cases depict a group of librarians trying to do the best they can. Protagonists exhibit both constructive and obstructive behavior. Some, however, mirroring real life, appear better than others. None is meant to represent a real person and any resemblance to living people is coincidental.

Thanks go to Barbara Adams for reading and offering insightful comments about the cases, to Caroline Coughlin for her sound advice and to Michele Armour for her technical assistance. The editorial pen of Irwin Gertzog deleted numerous hackneyed phrases and ill-conceived metaphors. For the errant judgments and inelegant constructions that remain, I, alone, bear responsibility.

# CASE ONE

## *CHOOSING SIDES*

A sociologist in her second year as a member of the Sequoia College faculty, Professor Rosalind McManus is seeking to have a Women's Studies major accepted into the curriculum. Her first year on campus was devoted to a number of activities designed to stimulate interest in the subject. She brought speakers to the College, helped students organize a group called SAGE, an acronym for Students Advocating Gender Equality, led weekly discussions focusing on feminist research which brought together male and female faculty members from a number of academic disciplines, and generally worked to raise consciousness about gender-related issues on campus. Among these were the frequency of date rape in the fraternity houses, the male-female stereotypes communicated to students by members of the career services office, and sexist language in the college newspaper. A conscientious teacher and a careful scholar, Professor McManus had won an active and dedicated following of students and apparent respect from faculty by the middle of her second year.

In light of the success of these ventures, Dr. McManus

judged that the time was right to approach the Curriculum Committee with a proposal that it adopt a Women's Studies major. The Curriculum Committee is one of the most important, prestigious and sought- after faculty assignments on the Sequoia Campus, and its membership generally includes established faculty luminaries and opinion-setters, and younger faculty being groomed to play those roles. Professor McManus considered herself well-prepared to present her ideas to the Committee. She had drafted descriptions of course requirements for the new major, adduced figures estimating the number of potential students who would enroll as majors, and compiled a list of faculty willing to teach part-time in the department. While anticipating some resistance to the proposal, she was unprepared for the outright antagonism and hostility she encountered from some members of the Committee, including Provost Courtenay Dodge.

Discussion centered on whether a Women's Studies program had the intellectual coherence to be considered legitimate. Members asked if it had the independent integrity to qualify as a discipline and, further, if there was a rigorous body of scholarly research associated with it. Among those who seemed to oppose the request were the Provost of the College - an ex-officio but nonetheless influential member of the Committee - and the Chairman of the History Department, who had similarly, and successfully, opposed a Black Studies major a decade before. Among the supporters were the Head of the Chemistry Department and the holder of the endowed chair in English. In true collegial fashion, the matter was discussed and, in the absence of apparent consensus, continued to a meeting the following month without a formal vote having been taken.

Regrouping, Professor McManus and her supporters resolved to mount an all-out campaign to educate students and faculty about the worthiness of their cause. They hoped that widespread, popular support would influence undecided Curriculum Committee members and that the weight of evidence might even change the minds of those who currently stood in opposition to the proposal. Among the important steps to be taken, Professor McManus decided, the first was to prepare a response to the two considerations which had surfaced during her presentation to the Curriculum Committee, the legitimacy of the discipline and its scholarly literature. She gathered data from other colleges and universities about whether they had Women's Studies Programs, and whether or not they also had subject majors. She learned that 125 colleges and universities offer Women's Studies majors on the undergraduate level, including such prestigious institutions as Yale and Harvard. This information, she hoped, would help to convince skeptics about the legitimacy of Women's Studies.

Her next action was to secure reading lists and bibliographies from Women's Studies courses and check the Sequoia Library OPAC and periodical holdings list to see how many of the books and journals were locally owned. To her disappointment, she found that the Sequoia Library contained few of the titles and that the monographs it did own were dated.

At this point Professor McManus quickly arranges to see Mike Nicholson, College Librarian, to make two requests. The first is that the library grant an emergency allocation of $12,000 in order to acquire 300 basic Women's Studies titles and 20 Women's Studies journals.

She tells him she will supply him with a list of titles. Second, she requests that the library place a display of these Women's Studies materials, as they are received, under a large sign in the lobby to highlight their arrival and their availability.

Nicholson is not unaware of the ongoing campus debate surrounding the Women's Studies proposal. It has become an emotional, albeit still minor campus issue. Proponents and opponents have felt the necessity to write heated letters to the student newspaper. Positions are rapidly crystallizing, as they tend to with most causes that emerge in late Winter or early Spring. Nicholson tells the young Sociology Professor that he will take the matter under advisement. "Suppose I make an appointment to see you early next week," Professor McManus suggests, "to learn what you have decided."

"Oh-oh," Nicholson thinks, "minefield," as Professor McManus exits his office. "Careful where you step...it may be on the toes of someone who will not or cannot support you." Nicholson wriggles deep into his padded chair, leans back, rests his laced fingers on his head, focuses on a tiny crack in the ceiling, and wishes he were once again spotting animals in the Masai Mara or witnessing the Son et Lumière show at Luxor.

Decisions like this, Nicholson is aware, are always complicated, and they have a way of producing consequences that are often only indirectly, if at all, related to the matter at hand.

Nicholson reviews the state of the current budget, as well as the one he has planned for next year. "I can shift funds. After all, it is only the middle of the fiscal year. But it probably means using all of my discretionary money for that purpose, or, alternately, going to departments to request their assistance. Some departments have spent their annual allocations already; others have scarcely touched theirs. The coffers of the History Department's book fund are still ample and I could ask them to part with a little of their capital, particularly since, in all probability, a number of the titles Dr. McManus will suggest have to do with women's history. But after Richard Friedberg's description at coffee this morning in the campus center about the scorn with which the Chairman of the History Department had explained the Women's Studies proposal, it would probably be wise to pursue an alternate route. In addition, *should* I meet Dr. McManus' request? *I* think a Women's Studies program is probably appropriate here at this time. But if the Curriculum Committee does not support a Women's Studies program, why should we invest in an expensive collection of books which may receive little or no use? Yet I want the faculty to think that the library is flexible and able to meet new and changing needs as they arise.

"Did she have to come to me the day after I delivered next year's budget request to the Provost's Office? And after I asked for a 10% jump up in the allocation so we can begin to have a decent collection of indexes and abstracts in CD-ROM. The prices they're charging! If the Provost sees me spending money to buy the Women's Studies materials for Dr. McManus, will she think I don't need the additional funds and decide not to support my new budget - particularly considering how she feels about the curriculum proposal?

"Has Professor McManus noted," Nicholson wonders,

"that the only display that has ever been placed in the center of the lobby is a life-sized soft-sculpture of a shopping-bag lady pushing a supermarket cart full of symbolic objects constructed by art students as part of a social conscience week. Not that I am against center lobby displays. But breaking precedent with a Women's Studies exhibit might be making a statement which perhaps the Library should refrain from articulating at this particular moment."

*                    *                    *

When Professor McManus comes back to see Librarian Nicholson, what will he tell her? What steps will he have taken in the interim? With whom will he have conferred? What are the additional questions he will have had to grapple with? What, if any, actions are required for damage control?

# CASE TWO

## *THE RIGHT PERSON*

Cora French, Director of the Weever College Library in Weever, Indiana, has been trying for three years to secure an additional professional staff position for the library. Now, after intensive lobbying and with the strong support of some members of the chemistry and biology departments, she has received permission to hire a science reference and bibliography librarian and to start that person at a higher salary than she would pay a recent library school graduate without the science credential. Feeling somewhat smug and self-satisfied, Cora knows that she will have on her staff the only science librarian in a 50-mile radius.

She begins her search by writing a job description that she can send to library schools and designs an advertisement that will appear in the *Chronicle of Higher Education* and *College and Research Library News*. She also plans to call associates in other libraries to see if they know of anyone in the market. This is the advertisement as it is carried in the two periodicals:

7

**WANTED:** Science reference librarian and bibliographer. Weever College Library, Weever, Indiana, 16335. Responsible for information services and collection development in Physics, Biology, Chemistry, Mathematics, Geology and other sciences. This includes liaison with faculty, students and researchers; specialized bibliographic instruction for printed and online sources; database searching; current awareness service. Qualifications: undergraduate degree in a science discipline, MLS from an accredited program. Second Master's desirable. Position available academic year beginning September. Salary range $25,000 - $28,000 depending on qualifications. Send résumé and names of three references to Science Librarian Search Committee, Weever College Library, Weever, Indiana 16335 by March 31. Weever College is an equal opportunity, affirmative action employer.

Cora next asks the Provost to name a search committee. At Weever, these committees generally have five members, one of whom is always the Provost, although he often plays an inactive role in the early committee work. Cora thinks that the committee should probably be composed of one member of the reference staff, the Provost, two scientists and herself. Her choice for the reference librarian slot is Diana Cowan, the woman who does the bulk of the online database searching as well as a good part of the bibliographic instruction. Unfortunately, Cora's choice for committee assignments is often Diana and she realizes it. But she trusts Diana's judgment more than that of the other members of the reference department. She forwards Diana's name and her own name to the Provost's Office with a note asking that he appoint two additional members to the search committee. To her surprise and delight, she learns that the Provost has named Neil Taylor, Chairman of the Chemistry Department and among the most influential members of the entire faculty, and Barbara Foster a junior but promising Physics Instructor.

Cora places the advertisement, makes her phone calls and waits for responses. Expecting a substantial response, she is disappointed when the applications only trickle in. By the appointed date, she has received seven, from which she immediately screens out three as clearly unqualified. She forwards all of the applications to committee members and summarizes for herself the applications of those she considers worthy of consideration. Of the four, she concludes that one is clearly outstanding and the other three average at best.

The following is Cora's summary of the candidates:

**Jane Smelton**, MLS, undergraduate high school mathematics. Graduate library school one and a half years ago. Letters of recommendation from teachers include such words or phrases as "adequate," "performs well with considerable direction," "quiet and unassuming." In her application letter, Jane indicates that she is looking for a position as a reference librarian and hopes that Weever will "seriously consider her application."

**Roscoe Smith**, Ph.D. Physics, ABD computer science, MLS. Letters indicate that Smith has taught at a number of institutions but has never earned tenure. Librarianship is his third profession. His recommendations include phrases such as "excellent researcher," "far and away the best paper-writer I have encountered in my years as a library school faculty member," "erudite, scholarly approach to science." Roscoe writes that he is sure that his extensive knowledge of physics will be a great asset to Weever, particularly his special expertise in high energy physics, where his familiarity with the literature is exceptional.

**Phyllis Lessinger**, MLS, undergraduate biochemistry. Her referees comment that while she was an average student, Phyllis was extremely well liked by both faculty and other students. One of the referees mentioned her particular skills with elementary school students, and added that Phyllis will be an excellent Children's Librarian. On her résumé, Phyllis has indicated that she seeks an interesting, entry-level library position. Phyllis's letter is terse and to the point. "I hope you will consider me for the position. If you have any questions, I can be reached at (908) 724-4558."

**Richard Blake**, MLS, MS Biology, undergraduate double major, psychology and chemistry. Richard's recommenders consider him to be "outstanding, conscientious, hardworking, friendly and well-motivated." In his well- written letter, Richard explains that he is particularly interested in Weever College as his long-range career plans include the directorship of a library at a quality liberal arts college. He explains that he finds university work less attractive since he is as interested in students as he is in collections. "

Gathering her papers, she sets out for the 4 o'clock Search Committee meeting. As she crosses the campus, Cora thinks about the candidates and their suitability for a job at Weever. "Richard is clearly the most outstanding applicant and should certainly be interviewed. Phyllis is probably worth inviting. I'd be willing to see the other two, but I must admit I don't have much enthusiasm for them." Noticing that the trees are almost in bud and that the rhododendron have lost their winter droop, Cora ruminates on how beautiful the campus is, the care it is given, how lucky the students are to be attending a fine institution such as Weever, and how attractive the campus will seem to a candidate despite its isolation from urban culture and its somewhat homogeneous student body.

Arriving at the meeting, she finds Taylor, Foster and the Provost, heads together, deep in whispered conversation. Diana is studying her notes, slightly uncomfortable at being excluded from the group. Cora is surprised to see the Provost since he normally waits until the time when final decisions are about to be made before taking part in meetings. Taylor suggests they start and that they consider each of the seven applications separately. Cora counters with the proposal that they eliminate all but the four candidates she finds acceptable. Taylor agrees, but adds that Richard's Blake's name should also be jettisoned. Aghast, Cora sputters," B..b..but he is the best of the bunch...Why would you dismiss him without even considering his qualifications?"

"I don't think he'll be happy here," counters Taylor.

"He is used to an urban environment."

"But he went to school at Bucknell," Cora responds, "and he knows where we are located. What makes you think he won't like it?"

"Well," says Taylor, "his activities seem to require a larger setting."

Bemused and alarmed, Cora wonders what Taylor is talking about, her eyes quickly scanning Richard's curriculum vitae. "Oh, damn, that's what it's all about," she thinks, noticing that Richard has run an AIDS information center in New Brunswick. "It didn't even occur to me that anyone might find that objectionable. It made him more attractive to me as a candidate because he had volunteered his professional services in a socially constructive way. I forgot that Taylor is such a rabid homophobe. It doesn't make any difference in any case, but I don't even know if Richard is gay. Now what do I do?"

Looking around the table, Cora tries to assess the position which each member might assume. Diana, of course, will support her. But she doesn't want to have the two librarians on one side and the rest on the other. The little she knows about Barbara Foster leads her to believe that she, too, may come down on the right side. But, given the young professor's relative newness on the faculty and her lack of tenure, Cora feels that she must try to avoid a split vote. The key is the Provost. How will he go? Is he sufficiently wary of Taylor's power to agree with him? Or can he be trusted to do the right thing.

"I'll push for an interview," decides Cora. "Maybe he will sell himself or perhaps he will prove to be unqualified. Either way we can defer the challenge." Accordingly she moves that the Committee agree to interview the four candidates she had originally chosen.

"Second," says the Provost.

        *            *            *

Assuming that after the interviews have been held, Cora considers Richard to be the ideal candidate, that Taylor is dead set against hiring him, and that the President of the College generally agrees with anything Taylor says, should Cora lobby for Richard's hiring? In framing a response, consider the legal and ethical dangers of discrimination on the basis of sexual preference, as well as the potentially negative impact the appointment may have on how a conservative Board of Trustees views the library's needs. Are there ways Cora can mollify Taylor, the President and others on the campus who may be hostile to Richard's hiring?

## CASE THREE

## *FIREBELL IN THE NIGHT*

The Bleeker College Library is a lovely Victorian building, octagonal in shape, with spiral staircases and marble balconies. Its reading rooms, lined with wood paneling, are entered through brass-handled, polished oaken doors. A smell of old books and aging leather, old varnish on oak tables greets the user. In truth, some complain that the room is musty and that the odor more closely resembles mildew than the classic aroma of antique paper and fine bindings.

Nonetheless the library has a quality that inspires nostalgia and warm feelings among alumni. To make reference to it in a request for contributions is to insure sums unattainable by appealing to the need for more dormitories or even a student center. No one is sure, least of all the development office, if it is because former students erroneously remember themselves as scholars during their time at Bleeker, because the library had been a favorite trysting place, or because libraries are simply totems that everyone feels should be supported.

"Oh God, how we need a new library," thought Bryan

Fields for the thousandth time, as he entered the general reference room to look up the price of the latest edition of Samuelson's economics text in *Books in Print*. "I just wish we didn't have to go through a formal needs assessment. I know we need a new library. The Committee knows we need a new library. The faculty knows we need a new library. Even the Administration knows we need one. Why can't we just get on with it? Dresser College somehow just found the money and so did Moorigan and their endowment, student body, even geographical location are similar to ours." Red-headed Bryan felt his face flush with the unspoken anger he was feeling. "I've been at them for years to build a new building. Just the insurance is costing us a fortune, but of course we can't do without it. The collection may go up in smoke any day, and to put a sprinkler system in would really blow the budget."

Bryan forgot his annoyance during a busy afternoon spent with trustees who had formed their own committee to look into the possibility of a new building. Excited at the prospect of creating a user-friendly structure with enough wiring to support all the technology he hoped to place in the new building, Bryan guided them through a crash course in the ramifications of database searching, OPAC, CD-ROM and other recent developments in the library field.

Regarding his afternoon as well spent, Bryan bolted down dinner - Lean Cuisine in the micro - so he could make his recorder group practice session on time. The evening disappeared in a rush of Vivaldi, Purcell and Bach. Once, in an unguarded moment, Bryan had told Earl Adams, Chairman of the Music Department, that he loved to play with his recorder group, that he found it so relaxing because during the time they played he thought of nothing else.  Of course it was true, but no professional likes to hear that an amateur finds "relaxing" the work he or she pursues so intensively.

Bed that evening was welcoming.  Two pages into the most recent issue of *College and Research Libraries*, Bryan's eyes crossed, then closed, and relaxed, dreamless sleep soon enveloped him.  A deep, whining noise followed rapidly by the shrill ring of the telephone forced his return to the waking world.  Rubbing his eyes, he sought to identify the sounds that had entered his consciousness. He put on his glasses and answered the phone.  "Bryan, this is Roscoe Collins, security.  There's a hell of a blaze in the library.  Could you get right over here?"

Now fully awake, his heart thumping, Bryan threw on his clothes and raced out the door.  The smell of smoke hung heavy in the air, even at his house, three-quarters of a mile from the library. Nearing the building, he saw thick billows spiraling upward.  Bryan spotted four engines on the scene, and just as he parked the car, the sirens renewed their plea for additional equipment and manpower.  He knew then that a disaster had occurred.

President Davis, eyes liquid from the smoke, stood watching the tongues of flame seek other parts of the building.  "I feel so helpless, Bryan," he admitted, "so damned frustrated."

"Did they get anything out?"  Bryan asked.

"The fire apparently started in the basement," Davis reported, "and they were able to get into the Treasure Room and save the manuscripts, most of the rare books and the Thomas Lincoln collection."

"What a relief," said Bryan. "That material is irreplaceable. The rest we can probably duplicate one way or another. Did they get the shelf list?"

"What's the shelf list?" Davis asked.

"The list of all the books we own, in the order they are shelved, that is, by their classification numbers," Bryan explained. "It was kept in technical processes in the basement."

"I doubt it," said Davis. "I know the card catalog went up like dry kindling. And that was on the first floor."

"It doesn't really matter. We can have the OCLC tapes run. I wonder whether they found the circulation files?"

"What good would that do?" asked Davis. "You still have to replace the entire collection. Listen, I've been thinking, you'd better move into Barrett Hall. It'll be makeshift, but at least you'll have a place to be. We'll delay renovation of the building for a career center until we figure out what to do about the library. It will be months, if not years. What will we do until then? Will the college have to close down? Can we possibly function without a library? What is a college without a library?"

Bryan sensed a hysterical note in Davis's voice as he

posed the questions. "That's real role reversal," he thought. "Davis is generally calming *me* down. And he's usually the soul of control, unflappable - even during sit-ins and student boycotts. I ought to find someone to take care of him so that I can survey the damage without having to worry about him as well."

Spotting Sam Edwards, who was currently serving as Dean of the Faculty, Bryan excused himself to the President and fought his way through the crowd. "Sam," he called. "Here. I need to talk to you."

Standing outside the earshot of faculty, students and others who were silently witnessing the firestorm, Bryan quickly explained the situation to Sam and suggested that he accompany President Davis, and when the President was willing to leave, see him home or take him to his own house for a stiff drink.

The flames began to diminish and suddenly, as if suffocated by a blanket, ceased entirely, with only an ember visible here and there. Bryan wandered around the building's periphery, peering through broken windows at the soaking shambles within. "Should we try the Florentine freeze-dried method?" he wondered. "Is it worth it? I'll locate some freeze-dry experts first thing in the morning."

From the fire chief Bryan sought to learn the extent of the destruction. The stacks were in the basement, and all of the materials there were a total loss. That included periodicals as well as books in all of the subject areas except for the art books, an exceptionally fine collection which had been housed in the Treasure Room. The general reference room had survived, but the reference books were covered with fire-fighting foam. It was unlikely that they could be salvaged. The microfilms had melted in their cabinets, so hot had been the fire. But, miraculously, in face of all probability, the circulation records had been rescued. "The only benefit," thought Bryan ruefully, "of having to place the circulation desk as close to the entrance and exit as possible. They must have gotten those files out immediately. Otherwise, they surely would have gone the way of the card catalog."

Slowly, the fire trucks began departing the scene, the crowds thinned out, and the faint light of tomorrow appeared on the horizon. Bryan climbed into his car to await the arrival of his staff. He had seen one or another of them at some time during the night, but most had now gone home, either to grab a cup of coffee or to change clothes.

While he desperately needed a new building, he felt that neither he nor his staff could cope with that project while attempting to rebuild the collection. "The collection has to be the focus," he concluded. "On the other hand, the insurance might give us a real start toward a new building."

\*       \*       \*

If you were Bryan Fields, what would you do today? tomorrow? next week? next month? next year?

In planning your actions, it is necessary first to address the questions that Davis has posed about the relationship between the college's program and the library.

Can a college function without a library? Is he correct in his conclusion that the collection must be his focus? Why was Bryan particularly anxious about the circulation files? How can research into library collection use help Bryan in his planning?

# CASE FOUR

## *MAPPLETHORPE AT McMILLAN*

Though short and blond, Eric Horne styles himself the William Buckley of McMillan College. His columns in the *Campus* are daily exposés of what he considers the "rotten underbelly" of the institution, and its liberal, godless, immoral and profligate ways. Few places on the campus have escaped his acid comment. The food service hires "dull-normals" incapable of making a BLT without scorching the bacon, and kowtows to food faddists who insist on salads and yogurt when "real men need good steak." Eric has castigated the faculty for their left-leaning political views, accusing them of trying to mold the student body in their image. He has fought what he considers the "good fight" against divestment of holdings in companies doing business with South Africa. McMillan trustees, primarily businessmen, also took Eric's position and voted not to divest, to the consternation and anger of the Black Student Alliance, the Young Democrats, the Students for Social Justice and the editorial board of the *Campus*.

Eric's latest target has been the Humphrey Library,

where he stumbled across the catalog of the Mapplethorpe photographic exhibit. **"Pornography in the Library,"** screamed the headline on his Monday column.

**Humphrey Library, in contradistinction to all established standards of morality and good taste, has chosen to purchase a volume of obscene and lascivious photographs, some of which depict naked children and others show acts of sado-masochism. This is the catalog of the infamous Mapplethorpe photographic exhibit. It should be recalled that the City of Cincinnati enjoined the Museum from displaying this very same exhibit and the Corcoran Gallery of Art in Washington cancelled its showing because of fear of retribution by the National Endowment for the Arts. Why should McMillan College be permitted to own and loan materials which violate community conventions and standards? In a democratic society citizens establish behavioral norms. The Supreme Court has given individual communities the right to decide for themselves what is contrary to public sensibilities. No one should have to be exposed to this shocking material. The library has demonstrated insensitivity and irresponsibility in selecting the Mapplethorpe catalog for its permanent collection. We demand that it be withdrawn immediately.**

Caroline Bennett, Director of the Humphrey Library, sat at her desk, sipping her morning coffee and reading the *Campus*. "It's nice to be included on Eric's Enemies List," she thought. The "we" in Eric's columns was always the royal "we" since he was known to be an isolate, without supporters or companions. "The Library is in good company this time. I only hope the Trustees don't take him too seriously. But they've always been good about academic and intellectual freedom. I wonder who'll answer Eric, or will I have to do it?"

Eric's columns always prompted a response, generally from a member of the faculty or the administration. This column's rejoinder came from Bob Czerni, Director of the Ebson Art Gallery and Professor in Photography and Art History, a fiery 1960s radical and ardent promotor of student and faculty rights. Bob's letter, full of righteous indignation, castigated Eric for his "know-nothing" attitude and his willingness to abrogate the principles of intellectual freedom in favor of censorship. He complained that despite Eric's enrollment in Art 421, Modern Photographic Masters, he had learned little about freedom of expression. Not even the Supreme Court, Bob contended, intended that works of "artistic merit" should be barred from sight and that "redeeming aesthetic value" always must outweigh community norms. And finally, the director of the Cincinnati Museum was exonerated by a jury of his peers. "Lighten up, Eric," he wrote. "You have nothing to lose but your conservatism and you might learn something in the process."

An exchange continued in the *Campus* over the next two weeks or so until Eric lost interest and focused his attention on the kind of entertainment being offered by the Student Center. Although most campus commentators agreed with Bob's position on the Mapplethorpe issue, there was consensus that he had damaged his case with his ad hominum attacks on Eric, and that if one were to judge the merits of the controversy solely on the written statements, Eric's argument would be adjudged by many as stronger.

Caroline was relieved that the issue had blown over without the Library becoming a political football, which was always a danger after one of Eric's attacks. The semester was winding down and to Caroline, a displaced New Yorker, the Library felt like a subway car at rush hour. Aggressive, anxious students fought their way to the Reference and Circulation desks demanding attention and service, or hovered over library tables and carrels, waiting for a place to become vacant. For staff, it was at once the best and the worst of times. The heady challenge of trying to answer three reference questions simultaneously stood in sharp contrast to the dismal exercise of repeating for the fortieth time where the addresses and committee assignments of members of the House of Representatives could be located.

Caroline had been helping out at the Reference Desk when she heard a loud, imperious voice above the constant buzz that suffused the library at this time of the term. "I *will* look at your records," the disembodied sound demanded. "I am a tenured faculty member at this institution and I have every right to know what a student has borrowed," it continued.

Excusing herself from the sophomore she had been helping, Caroline rushed up to the front lobby to find Bob Czerni pounding his fist on the circulation desk. Offering her hand in welcome, she calmly said, "Hello, Professor Czerni." The act of shaking hands seemed to soothe Bob, and Caroline continued, "Perhaps we can talk in my office."

"Now, how can I be of help?" asked Caroline as Bob settled into her office couch and she seated herself behind her desk.

"I just received this paper from Eric Horne," he explained, "and I know...I am simply positive...that it is plagiarized. He could not have written with such authority and clarity on the subject. And besides, the views are not Eric's. The paper applauds contemporary, minimalist photography, asserting that the form frees artists from traditional constraints and permits them to concentrate on what is essential. Can you imagine Eric writing that?"

"I can't," replied Caroline. "It certainly doesn't sound like his usual line."

"Well, I asked the student behind the desk to look through the circulation records to see what Eric had checked out recently so I can examine the sources he may have used to write his paper. She refused, saying it was against library policy. Would you please arrange that for me?"

"The student is correct," said Caroline. "No one can see what has been borrowed by anyone. That is indeed our policy. Surely you can understand that it protects us all."

"I can understand the need to protect faculty privacy," countered Bob. "But in case you didn't know, it is also the policy of this institution that plagiarism is illegal. If proven, it is grounds for instant dismissal. Surely, faculty are special and can be trusted to handle these records carefully and with circumspection. Oh, how I'd love to catch that Horne cheating!" Bob rose, expecting to be led to the records.

"I'm sorry," Caroline responded firmly, her own voice now tinged with anger at his refusal to listen to her. "That particular policy is inviolate."

"It is your obligation to help me locate plagiarism. I demand to see your records, and if you won't help, I'll go to the Provost. I know he will support me," Bob threatened.

"Then you'll have to go to the Provost," Caroline retorted angrily, "because you're not going to see those records."

"I'll be back..soon," an irate Bob promised, as he left her office.

True to his word, Bob was back with Provost Jonathan Nesbitt within the hour. "I understand Bob has made a request to see some circulation records, Caroline," said Jonathan. "Plagiarism is very serious, and besides that, Eric is such a pain in the butt. Make an exception. No one will ever know."

*          *          *

How does Caroline now respond to the Provost?

# CASE FIVE

## *SIX GOES INTO FIVE HOW MANY TIMES?*

Stuyvesant College, a branch of the City University of New Chicago, is experiencing the same budget shortfalls as other city services have felt during the past fiscal year. Despite the best efforts of Mayor Dalkins to find funds under every high-rise and in every corporate nest, the city's economy is still in dire straits, with no relief in sight.

"The Reagan legacy strikes again," thinks Cliff Owens, head librarian at the college library. "Every social and cultural program has felt the pinch in these last few years. The trickle down effect has finally reached this library."

The Stuyvesant College Library has been known throughout the urban college library community as an exemplary institution. Cliff's well-earned reputation is based, among other reasons, on his willingness to experiment, to try new ideas, to be in on the beginning of things. The Library, for instance, was the first academic institution in the area to offer on-line data base searching, and was the first to install an integrated automated system.

27

Also well-known is Cliff's ability to attract a talented group of staff members. Newly minted professionals, eager for the experience of working at the Stuyvesant College Library, have been willing to settle for substantially lower starting salaries than they might be offered elsewhere. Dan Clark, a graduate of UNC Library School, and now Associate Director of the Oberlin College Library, recalls ruefully how he left the Stuyvesant College Library, despondent after his interview but knowing that he would take the position there if it were offered to him, even though other colleges were prepared to pay him $3,000 more than the Stuyvesant job paid.

When speaking to library school classes about his personnel practices, Cliff has reported that although he is willing to be a mentor, what he tries hardest to achieve is to give staff members the ability to act independently. "In other words," he told the students, "I try to find good people, build on their strengths, and let them go as far as these strengths will take them." The major personnel problem which Cliff faced from time to time was having to encourage librarians to leave a comfortable home in the Stuyvesant Library to seek jobs with more responsibility.

"I'm luckier than some," thought Cliff, scrutinizing his budget for the coming year. "I've automated; and I'm about to have a retirement. At least I don't have to fire anyone. No way could I have kept six professionals on staff with the 5% I must cut. But now I have to rewrite the job descriptions to cover all the work that has to be done."

Cliff pulled out his staff manual, turned to the organization chart and opened the looseleaf binders. He removed the chart and the six pages of job descriptions which followed and photocopied them. After replacing the originals in the manual, he spread the copies out across his desk, located a pair of scissors and got ready to shuffle and cut and paste.

"I know that organization charts do not create good organizations," Cliff thought. "On the other hand, they can act as stumbling blocks and stand in the way of getting things accomplished."

Cliff reviewed the six professionals currently serving on the staff, thought about their responsibilities and backgrounds, and assessed their abilities.

Here is the chart as it stood:

[See page 30]

ORGANIZATION CHART

PROFESSIONAL STAFF

STUYVESANT COLLEGE

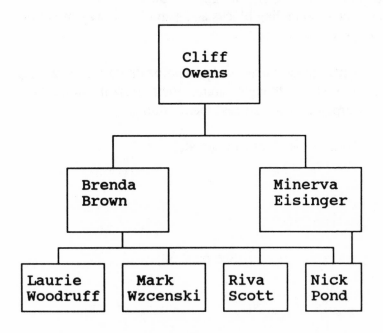

BRENDA BROWN: 65, Assistant Director/Reader Services, retiring Humanities and general reference librarian. On staff for 31 years, ever since her graduation from University of Chicago Library School. Clips *New York Times* and *Chistian Science Monitor* for vertical file each day and is the only one who knows where anything in the vertical file is. Has a sound group of supporters in the Humanities departments, particularly in English. Brenda has willingly worked fourteen hours each weekend and has also covered one evening. Rarely takes vacation. Oversees collection development in Humanities.

"Can't say I'm sorry she's leaving," thought Cliff. "In her day, she must have been superb. But technology has left her in the dust. And she's become so squirrely with that vertical file collection. If she's not around, nobody can find a thing."

LAURIE WOODRUFF: 28, reference librarian. Her science background makes her the favorite of physicists, chemists, biologists and mathematicians. Enthusiastic, bright, energetic. On staff for one year, since her graduation from UC Berkeley. Anxious to take advantage of New Chicago, Laurie has been professionally active outside the library, serving as membership chair of the METRO college librarians. She also reviews books for *Choice*. A promoter of the concept of Information Literacy, Laurie has been working with Susan Day of the English department to incorporate a new approach into the freshman writing program. Laurie shares responsibility with Cliff for keeping the science collections up to date.

"She is a comer. I'll have her out of here in three years, into a quality liberal arts institution. She knows

how to talk to faculty; her reference interviewing skills are
the best on staff; and she watches the reviewing media like
a hawk to fill in gaps in our collection. I just have to be
careful not to overload her."

MARC WZCENSKI: 40, reference librarian. Supervisory
responsibility for audiovisual, interlibrary loan and
periodicals. On staff seven years, since his graduation
from Drexel. Has three master's in addition to library
science degree. A gifted musician, he sometimes leaves
the impression he'd rather be blowing his saxophone than
answering reference questions. Marc is conscientious,
quiet and somewhat self-effacing. He is attentive to
students and faculty, but finds it difficult to make eye
contact. His constituents are musicians and other fine
artists. His collection development areas are fine arts,
music and audio-visual materials.

"I'm sorry not to have done better for you, Marc,"
thought Cliff. "You should've been out of here by now,
as Associate or even Head Librarian somewhere. But you
don't seem too interested. Perhaps I need to give you
more management responsibility. Maybe I'll let you do
the preliminary budget for next year. At least you'll have
that experience."

RIVA SCOTT: 28, reference librarian. Chiefly
responsible for on-line data base searching. Interested in
bibliographic instruction. Came to Stuyvesant four and a
half years ago. Extremely intelligent, progressive,
well-trained at Michigan - both at Library School and in
the University Library. Respected by students and faculty.
Has a dedicated following in the biology department.
Major drawback, painfully thin, probably anorexic,

resulting in diminished energy and frequent illness. She is in charge of materials in the Life Sciences, those in biology and psychology.

"Ah, Riva. What am I going to do with you? You are the kind of librarian the field needs. You've got super training, you're capable of seeing the big picture, understanding the new developments. Yet, you've gotten too comfortable here and I think you're fearful of putting yourself in the job market. Not without reason. An institution would be afraid to hire you with the potential health problems your anorexia may bring on."

NICK POND: 30, splits his work between cataloging and reference. On staff for one and half years. Well-liked by students and faculty, Nick is competent and thorough, but only does what he is asked. His chief following is among business faculty and majors, especially those in investment analysis with whom he likes to talk about market fluctuations and precious metals. Nick is patient when doing bibliographic instruction, although his approach is traditional, beginning with the card catalog and continuing to the *Reader's Guide*. Is responsible for social sciences materials in economics, political science and sociology.

"I can't tell if you're going to make it, Nick. Your work is good, but you can't seem to go beyond the minimum limits of your job. Use your imagination; do something innovative. All that literature they fed you in library school about pro-activity, and still you can only react. Well, you're still new. Perhaps you'll grow and develop."

MINERVA EISINGER: 43, Head cataloger. Bright,

capable. On staff for two years, following husband's decision to leave Cleveland State for New Chicago after a fight with the Provost there. Minerva does her work well, supervises Nick Pond and lends encouragement, confidence and expertise to Technical Processes.

"What a find you are, Minerva. I know I only have you because Greg decided to come here and that I will only keep you as long as he likes Stuyvesant."

The Library at Stuyvesant College is open 95 hours a week when school is in session. This includes 15 hours a day from Monday through Friday, and ten hours each on Saturday and Sunday. It is assumed that at least one professional staff member will be on duty during each hour that the library is open, including weekends and evenings. The Stuyvesant College faculty is responsible for selecting materials for the library in subject disciplines, but the staff chooses reference, audio-visual, and periodical materials, and oversees the rest of the collection, as well. All members of the reference staff do some bibliographic instruction.

*     *     *

Based on your knowledge of the professional tasks which must be accomplished in a college library, and on your assessment of the abilities of the current staff of the Stuyvesant College Library as described by Cliff Owens, design a new organization chart and write job descriptions for each member of the staff. Then formulate a plan for reporting to the staff what you have designed and why. Remember that Cliff is open-minded and would entertain nontraditional paths to achieving appropriate staffing.

# CASE SIX

## *THE TOWER OF KNOWLEDGE*

Jim Kramer, still youthful and uncommonly good-looking at 68 years old, serves with enthusiasm as chairman of the Spenser College Trustees' Development Committee. A loyal alumnus, his successful career has included ownership of the Yankee Bottling Company (which he sold at a $20 million profit) and Mueller's Cake Treats, an Eastern-based bakery specializing in Devil Twists and Footlongs, two kinds of chocolate pastries consumed mostly by children. Self-effacing about his accomplishments, Kramer has been known to respond with Woody Allen's now famous aphorism when asked the secret of his success: "Ninety per cent of life is just showing up."

Despite his reluctance to boast, Kramer is a formidable contender in any arena and has been enormously effective as a fund-raiser for the college. Always willing to prime the pump for any new undertaking, he has recently launched the drive to raise $8 million dollars for a new library by contributing $980,000 as seed money. Furthermore, he contends that most of the $7 million-plus necessary to complete the project will be in the college's

35

coffers by early Spring, so that groundbreaking can be held no later than July.

"Considering that November is almost over," thought Mack Slater, Director of the Spenser College Library, "that would be close to impossible if Kramer were not spearheading the campaign. But I have complete faith in his ability to make good on his word. Thank goodness I have the building program written and the building committee in place. According to campus talk, when he decides to do something, you'd better be ready or it's good-bye. Many heads have rolled over a Kramer project."

Mack's thoughts were interrupted by his Secretary's voice on the intercom. "Jim Kramer on line one," she announced.

"Hello, Mr. Kramer," said Mack.

"Good to talk to you, Slater," the voice on the line boomed. "I'd like to see you this Thursday afternoon, if that's possible for you. The Trustees' meeting is Friday, and if you can meet with me, I'll fly in on Thursday morning. I've got some things about the Library to discuss with you. Are you available?"

Checking his calendar, Mack noted that he had a meeting scheduled with the Vice-President for Operations Research to talk about hooking dorm rooms and faculty offices into the library's OPAC. Certain that Sherman will understand the need to rearrange the meeting, Mack told Kramer he would make himself available and they agreed to meet at two.

Prior to the meeting, Mack carefully selected a number of materials about building college libraries that he considered useful to their discussion. He had amassed a great deal of information in the course of writing the building program and felt that he was knowledgeable about the important considerations in academic library construction. In addition, he was excited about the prospects of a new library, having put up with inadequate quarters during the three years he has been at Spenser.

On Thursday afternoon, Mack straightened his office, retied his tie, made sure his Secretary knew that coffee would be required, and left instructions with her that he was not to be interrupted during Kramer's visit.

Promptly at two o'clock the Secretary announced Kramer's arrival. Mack made a quick appraisal of the man as they shook hands. Those incredible steely blue eyes, he thought with some amusement, are sizing me up just like I'm trying to get a fix on him. He's probably better at it. Knows just how far he can push me. All I know at first glance is that I would hate to be on the opposite side of any position he takes.

"Won't you sit down?" Mack asked. "Can I get you some coffee?"

"No thank you," Kramer responded. "Just finished lunch. The President insisted I meet Bob Billington, the newspaper publisher, and I had one of those Country Club salads which they advertise as being healthy and non-fattening, but are so big that they could feed a whole African village. These trips out here are midriff threatening.  I always have to run an extra mile for two weeks after a trip to Pleasantville.  Listen, would you tell your Secretary that Rick Bostick is expected momentarily.  You've met Rick Bostick, haven't you?  The architect?"

"I'm afraid not," answered Mack, "but, of course I know who he is.  I was in the Coliseum Tower last week to see the Classic Car Show.  It's some construction.  He's an amazing architect.  You can see the influence of Philip Johnson, of Frank Lloyd Wright and of Noguchi, but the feeling is different.  I would certainly love to meet him.  What is he doing at Spenser?"

"Well, he belongs to my Club at home and I called him last week to ask if he'd ever done a library.  He told me he never had, but would love to.  We had lunch on Friday and he came up with the notion of building a Learning Tower - ten stories high.  I think it's a sensational idea.  The President tells me the new library will be placed right in the center of the college.  What could better symbolize the library as the heart of the community than a large vertical structure visible from any part of ..."

Kramer was stopped in mid-sentence by the Secretary's announcement that Bostick had arrived and was on his way in.  Mack and Kramer both rose to greet the world-renowned architect.

"Beautiful campus," commented Bostick, as Mack motioned him to a chair.  "Grey stone utilized in the new library would continue tradition, even in a modern structure.  I'm a great believer in the importance of tradition."

Talking about the campus and its structures led easily into a discussion of the new library. Mack distributed copies of the building program to Kramer and Bostick, although he was sure the former had already received one from the President. He led them through it, pointing out space requirements for collections, staff and patrons. He explained the importance of creating a user- friendly structure which could be properly serviced by the staff he had available.

Kramer and Bostick nodded politely in agreement, but Mack sensed a certain impatience on their parts. "I can't blame them," he thought, "those are details which interest librarians, but have little meaning for them."

Finally, Kramer could contain himself no longer. "Rick," he said, "show Mack the preliminary sketches you drew up." Rick unfolded his drawings, spread them out on the conference table and explained them to Kramer and Mack.

"Aren't they sensational?" asked Kramer, when Rick had finished. "What do you think about the Learning Tower, Mack? Isn't it a stupendous idea? This ten-story Library will be the talk of the academic community. It will win prizes and be featured in the *Architectural Record*. I can hardly wait to get started. I might add that the President is equally excited."

"He's really serious," Mack realized with a shock. "At first I thought he was just speculating about the possibility of building a Tower. He's right, of course. We will be the talk of the academic community. Everyone will be laughing at us. No tower has ever served an academic library well. It's wrong for collection development, for supervision, for staffing, and generally for use. How do I tell him this without jeopardizing the project? And what if he doesn't listen to me?"


         *             *             *


Why is Mack so set against a tower? Can his assertions be documented? Is there evidence he can bring to bear? Where can he look for allies and support?

## CASE SEVEN

# EQUAL OPPORTUNITY FOR STUDENTS WITH UNEQUAL POCKETBOOKS

Ruth Cotton, Librarian of the Dayton State College Library, strode to the check-out desk.

"What's going on?" she demanded of Fred Rider, head of circulation, who was in a heated argument with a student.

"It's not fair," said senior Stella Edwards, pointing to two stacks of books in front of her. "I simply can't afford to pay $1.00 each just to borrow those 12 interlibrary loan books. It's not as if they're overdue."

Ruth looked through the piles as Fred and Stella continued to press their claims.

"But that's the rule," insisted Fred. "It is written right here in the library's policy manual. You can't have those books until you pay for them."

"I didn't even know about the policy," Stella countered. "The student who helped me didn't say anything about it. But even if I had known, I probably

41

would have requested them anyway. I need those materials to finish my honors thesis. And you don't have anything on the subject. Look, I'll pay you when my student aid check comes through, OK?"

"Sorry," said Fred. "The Business Manager has put his foot down on credit. You can't even charge at the bookstore anymore. He says that the default rate is so high that the College can no longer afford to let students defer payments. We'll hold your books for a week. Then we'll send them back."

"Library staff taking interlibrary loan requests are responsible for warning students that there will be a fee. If you weren't informed of your obligation, then perhaps we should waive the charge in this case, Ruth suggested, trying to ameliorate the situation.

Though obviously reluctant and visibly annoyed, Fred agreed to Ruth's solution. After the transaction had been completed, Ruth proposed that she and Fred have a cup of coffee in the staff lounge.

They sat in silence, Ruth mindlessly stirring her coffee, until Fred could contain himself no longer. "You always side with students and faculty against the staff," he accused her. "You could see that she was on a fishing expedition with those books she ordered. Why did she need 12? Why couldn't it have been two or three? And why didn't she pick a topic where the material would be available here? Students just take advantage every chance they get."

Ruth knew how upset Fred was and how he was

reflecting staff perceptions about students. She just wished he would gain a little more maturity and not act quite so peevish. He wanted to go to library school, and eventually become a reference librarian. But he would have to grow up, develop patience for students and learn to hold his tongue.

"She probably was just browsing in those interlibrary loan books," agreed Ruth. "Some of them looked more like self-help manuals than empirical studies of post-Freudian short-term therapy. Someone should have steered her to reviews before she went ahead and ordered the books. On the other hand, it is true that our collections in that area are not what they should be."

They chatted for a while about other student excesses, about problems Fred was having with one of his clerical workers, about how good the current crop of student assistants seemed to be, and about whether Dayton State would advance to the Division III NCAA regional basketball finals. When she judged Fred to be sufficiently calm, she excused herself and settled into an afternoon of grant request writing. She had been offered the papers of a former senator, a graduate of Dayton State College, which she very much wanted to accept. But she needed additional funds to organize, describe and preserve the collection. A conversation with the Fidelity Trust Foundation had given her the encouragement and motivation she needed to write the request for funds.

Two days later Ruth found in her mail an intra-campus letter from Bill Anderson, Chairman of the Psychology Department, requesting that she bring to the attention of the Library Committee his request that the Library make available to all students without charge any interlibrary loan materials they may wish to borrow. He explained that Stella Edwards had complained to the department about the Library's charge policy. He was surprised to learn that the Library levied a fee for this service. He had asssumed, "based apparently on no information whatsoever," that the Library granted students the same unlimited ILL access as it did to faculty. He reminded her that she had assured him that materials they did not purchase were available through DAYNET.

"Did your assurance cover only faculty? At our school in particular, with so many students on tight budgets, and a great disparity between the haves and have-nots, it seems singularly short-sighted to charge for this kind of service. What it means is that if you have the money, you have an advantage over a student who cannot afford the fee. Raise the price of toothpaste and candy bars in the bookstore, but don't chase students away from anything which encourages learning. Thank you for your attention to this matter. I look forward to receiving a favorable response."

Ruth's first impulse was to be annoyed with Stella Edwards for complaining to Bill Anderson; her second was to be annoyed with Bill Anderson for forcing her to take his complaint to the ineffective Library Committee. Both annoyances faded with the realization that little time remained before the next Library Committee meeting and she would be better served by gathering good information than by indulging herself in pointless resentment. She began by hunting down last year's ILL statistics and assessing how much funding would be required to meet student demand for material from other libraries.

She had borrowed about 5,500 books for students during the last academic year, but she knew that the number of requests would double if the service were to be offered free. Although the student charge was $1.00, the real cost to the library was closer to $2.00. That would mean $22,000 for student ILLs, an additional $11,000 over this year's expenditure. "The money's just not there," she thought. "I simply cannot afford to support student interlibrary loan."

The Dayton State College Library Committee met in the Library on the fourth Thursday of each month at four o'clock. Meetings always began late and ended by five. What ensued in between could best be summarized by, in Ruth's words, "Bo-o-o-ring." Committee Chair Gerry Rodgers insisted on having the minutes of last month's meeting read aloud. Given Carol Hanson's propensity for noting every statement made by a committee member, ten minutes were devoted to this exercise. A review of the monthly library statistics and financial statement consumed an additional 25 minutes. When Ruth finally read Bill's letter to the group and reported her position on the matter, based on the strain that providing free ILL would put on the budget, a scant fifteen minutes were left for discussion. Moments of silence followed. "Perhaps it's just my perception," thought Ruth, "but they seem uncomfortable with what I've said. That's strange. They almost always support me. The only time they disagreed was about the right of students to have a smoking corner in the all-night study."

Finally Gerry broke the ice. "I think we ought to do it for the students," he said. "Dr. Anderson's position makes good sense, particularly at this institution, with what we are trying to accomplish."

"But where will we find the money?" asked Ruth.

"Perhaps we could ask the departments to pick up the tab," suggested Carol. "Or we could require students to have a faculty member's signature in order to borrow a book. That way they wouldn't take advantage."

"I could live with either of those solutions," responded Ruth. "As a matter of fact, I think they'll work well together. Students will be required to have the faculty member who is advising a paper OK the request and that department will be charged for the loan."

The Library Committee, noting five o'clock, took a hurried vote and directed Ruth to inform Bill Anderson of its decision.

*          *          *

Do you think the college library committee has embarked on a wise course? What are some of the ramifications of its decision?

CASE EIGHT

## *THE SPOUSE ON THE STAFF*

Pomfret College makes its home in Pomfret, a small community in southern West Virginia located 120 miles south of Pittsburgh, 200 miles east of Cincinnati, and 125 west of Richmond. Local wits call it "centrally isolated." Despite its rural location, Pomfret boasts a national reputation based on the excellence of its teaching faculty and its commitment to non-traditional approaches to education. Its students are as likely to be from Chicago or Denver as from nearby Charleston.

Libby Peters, newly appointed head librarian of the Pomfret College Library and in her first directorship, chose to take the Pomfret job despite offers by larger and better endowed institutions because of the apparent willingness of faculty to use the library's resources and make them an integral part of the college's educational program. Students are exposed to instruction in library use from the moment they enter Pomfret until completion of their senior projects. Unlike most small liberal arts institutions, Pomfret's Library has a well-developed manuscript and rare book collection, housed in a wood-paneled Treasure Room with inlaid floors and oak cabinets. The manuscript collections of the early feminist, Mary Fredericks, 19th-century Governor Rich DesPlante, author Robinson Carter, and botanist Charles Fleming, all alumni of Pomfret, have been placed there. In addition, there is a rare book collection of early American imprints relating to the settlement of the Western Reserve. Students are encouraged, under supervision, to do original research using the documents and books.

As her first hire, Libby must find a part-time, rare book-manuscript librarian to replace Sally Hodkins who is leaving to work at Beinecke, Yale's rare book library, while pursuing a doctoral degree in Medieval History. Hodkins, a recent divorcée, is the ex-wife of the principal of Pomfret High School, and discovered her historical interest while ranging through the Treasure Room collections. The job is a non-professional one and pays just over minimum wage.

"It won't be easy to find a replacement," Libby lamented, as she wrote the ad which would appear in the Pomfret *Tribune* and in the campus newspaper. "Sally was intelligent, efficient and interested. I can't imagine a Pomfret high school graduate having the same qualifications."

To her surprise and pleasure, Libby received a letter of application from Virginia Cooper, wife of Jim Cooper, head of the Mathematics Department. A trained archivist, skilled in preservation, Virginia had worked with manuscripts and rare books at Stanford University and Vassar College. English by birth, she has no American credentials and is therefore ineligible for most "professional" library jobs.

"What a find!" thought Libby, as she called Virginia for what she considered a pro forma interview. "I know I can't possibly unearth a better candidate here in Pomfret."

Libby met with Virginia on a Monday morning. The encounter was as satisfying as she has anticipated. Virginia knew the rare book market, was familiar with out-of-print dealers, understood acidity problems and, best of all, had reviewed the collection and was prepared to make recommendations about what needed to be done to organize and preserve it. Without a further attempt to recruit candidates for the position, Libby offered it to Virginia. She was gratified when it was accepted on the spot.

The following Monday Virginia began work. Libby gave her an abbreviated orientation and set her loose in the Treasure Room, looking in at least once a day. After two weeks, on a Friday morning Libby paid Virginia an extended visit.

"How's it going, Virginia?" she inquired. "Any major problems?"

"Oh, no," responded Virginia. "Everything is wonderful. I've got a good idea what the collection contains, and have set up rules for the use of manuscripts and rare books."

"What kind of rules?"

"Oh, you know," said Virginia, opaquely.

"No, I don't. Rules in this library are generally made with the participation, or at least the approval, of the Library Director. What have you put into effect?"

"Did you know that my predecessor let *students* use manuscripts - and early American imprints?" she asked.

"Of course she did," Libby responded. "This library prides itself on helping students do original research from primary sources."

"But documents get dirty, and they are fragile," Virginia asserted. "I've got a long-range plan to microfilm all of the documents, and when that's completed, students can utilize them for research," she added, obviously trying to placate Libby.

"Microfilms aren't the same as original manuscripts," countered Libby. "In addition to their being second-generation and dependent on good camera-work, students lose all sense of history without the tactile feel of 19th-century paper and the visual effect of a quill pen or a stylus. I understand your concern for the material, but under your supervision students will learn respect for the material and how to use it properly," Libby said, appealing to Virginia's obvious respect for good manners and behavior. "Why don't we talk about it next Monday, after we've both had the opportunity to consider the issues involved. Three o'clock in my office?"

Dinnertime in the Cooper household was always preceded by sherry hour and a review of the day's events.

"You look troubled, Virginia," Jim observed.

"Oh, that new head librarian fell off my fork today," Virginia responded. "She simply doesn't know what she's doing. She has the mentality of an undergraduate." Virginia proceeded to describe to Jim the morning's exchange.

"I'm sure she'll see it your way," counseled Jim. "Just go about your job."

"No, I think she's determined, Jim," Virginia declared.

Saturday evening found the Coopers at a party in honor of Josh Bennett's newly achieved tenure. As usual, campus gossip won out over other topics of conversation and attention was soon focused on Virginia's reports on the library and the incompetence of the new librarian.

Sunday, after chapel, Virginia walked home with Kate Wylie, professor of political science, and once again reported that the library was in trouble, that students held sway and the library's precious resources were in jeopardy. On Monday, she had lunch with Marjorie Cristos, wife of the Chairman of the English department, and couldn't help but comment on the librarian's lack of intellect. The intermission at Donald Cronin's piano concert on Wednesday gave her an opportunity to inform still others of library events. And Thursday's cocktails at the President's to meet a visiting scholar provided her with her most important listener.

In the meantime, Libby, oblivious to the campaign against her, had drawn up a list of reasons why students should be permitted direct access to the manuscript collections. Utilizing statements from a number of well-known librarians from institutions such as Amherst, Smith and Wesleyan to support her conclusion, she intended to convince Virginia without calling on her authority as head of the library.

In the morning of the day she was to have met with Virginia, she was visited by the Provost, the Head of the English Department, a well-respected political scientist, and the Chaplain. All seemed solicitous of her welfare. They asked if she was happy at Pomfret, whether there have been unexpected problems in the library, and whether the students are difficult to work with, among other probing questions. This sudden burst of concern makes evident to Libby that there were underlying but unstated reasons for their visit. When the President's secretary called to set up an appointment, she was convinced that something was wrong. A call to Jack Roberts, chair holder in history and one of the few real friends she had made at Pomfret, revealed the damage to the library and to her that Virginia has managed to inflict during the week since their initial conversation. Libby must think quickly about what to say to Virginia that afternoon. And then she must turn her attention to the difficult task of regaining the respect and confidence of the college community.

*          *          *

How will this be accomplished?

# CASE NINE

## *THE HONOR CODE AND THE RESERVE BOOK ROOM*

"I wish the faculty would be a little more imaginative in the way they make assignments, so that we can clean out the reserve shelves," lamented David Jenkins, Director of the Orangeville, Oregon, College Library. He was reading a report submitted to him by the circulation staff, which had analyzed reserve material use over the past three years. "Those reserve shelves are bulging with unused books. Students read only two or three of the items that faculty assign. And the rest gather dust. I've got to find some way to de-select some of them or they'll end up in piles on the floor."

David emitted a tuneless little hum, which he heard in his mind as "My Boy Bill" from Rodgers and Hart's *Carousel*. Humming under his breath, an unpleasant habit he had developed while in college, surfaced when he was preoccupied or attempting to solve a problem. Even the staff was alert to the meaning of the monotone sounds and knew that on the day they could be heard, David's attention to their needs would be negligible.

The staff's report, labeled with a large

"CONFIDENTIAL" on the cover, first presented a statistical narrative describing the use made of all reserve materials. It read:

**Four thousand books were placed on reserve for 200 courses offered by 100 faculty members. They were circulated 16,000 times, or an average of four per book, compared with an average of 15 students per course. Of the 4,000 books on reserve, 3,000 never circulated, putting the average circulation of every used volume at sixteen.**

**The following faculty members have placed more than 20 books for each of their courses on reserve: Gleason of German, Scott of Psychology, Combretti of Physics, Goldstone, Heinrich, and Carroll of English, Raybuck and Duhamel of Political Science, Madison of Art and Smith, Murphy, Testa, Francis and Bleighstone of History. In not one of their courses were more than 25% of the titles on the reserve list used. In most, 10% or less circulated.**

**We request that Mr. Jenkins speak to the faculty or the administration about this situation.**

**Respectfully submitted,**
**Marlene Sessions, Jeff Hanahan, Bob Keough**

Orangeville College is a Quaker School that boasts a tradition of civility and consensus building when tackling campus problems. David sometimes found the endless discussion of issues "in community" tedious, his East Coast impatience combining with a somewhat authoritarian approach to getting things done. Yale, where he had done his undergraduate work, had not prepared him for the egalitarian atmosphere which pervaded Orangeville. From Washington, D.C. he had acclimated to Yale by adopting its tone, posture, and pace, though not the elitist attitudes he encountered in some undergraduates, alumni and a few faculty. Unfortunately, a flippant tone and his tendency to make judgmental asides gave faculty, students and administrators at Orangeville the impression that not only was he an "Easterner" (meaning uppity) but somewhat arrogant, as well. His staff knew otherwise. They ignored his tendency to "fire" before he was ready - or before he had even taken aim - because they knew he would eventually come to not only a good decision, but the right one. Some faculty were adjusting, as well.

The library job at Orangeville was a plum. The institution had a reputation of excellence unparalleled by all but a few liberal arts colleges, none of which would have offered him the Head Librarian position after only four years in the Reference Department at Hamilton College. His mentor at Columbia, where he had completed his MLS and performed brilliantly, even under circumstances of institutional uncertainty and impending doom, had urged him to take the job, but had warned him that he would have to learn to be judicious in his utterances. "Speaking, in this case, David," he warned, "must not be merely thinking aloud."

By now David had switched to "I Feel Pretty" from
*West Side Story*, although no one but David could
distinguish between it and his previous selection.   The
question is, he thought, would it be best to write
individual notes to the faculty about the reserve books, to
speak with the Provost and have her bring it up for
discussion at the next faculty meeting, or merely to meet
informally and individually with all of the people whose
lists have been identified as over-long and under-used?
Each method seemed fraught with peril at Orangeville.  At
Hamilton we could simply have said we were removing all
books which have not circulated from the reserve shelf.
Here you don't do that.  Not so much because no  faculty
member wants to be told that students are not fulfilling
their assignments, and not because the reserve lists are so
old that students no longer find the material relevant, but
because so abrupt an approach is incompatible with
community consensus building.

His concentration was interrupted by a tap on his
office door.   Gustave, Heinrich, one of the English
professors whose name appeared on the circulation staff's
list, peeked around the doorway.

"Do you have a minute, David?" he asked.

"Sure, Gus, come in."

David enjoyed a particular relationship with Gustave,
who had completed his graduate studies at Yale.   They
both could bemoan a fate which placed them so far from
the tables down at Maury's and shared a nostalgia for a
particular reading nook in Sterling Library.  Beyond that,

they had little in common. Gustave was known on the campus as a Puritan - moral, self-righteous, eager to make students toe the line, and punitive when they did not, no matter how slight the infraction. A student paper turned in an hour later than it was due always commanded a grade less than it would have earned on its merits, no matter the extenuating circumstances.

"A serious problem has come to my attention," Gustave began. "Some students in my class have reported that two other members of that class have been keeping reserve materials not only beyond the time they are due, but past the time of the examinations that cover materials contained in them. I think this is a serious violation of the honor code, don't you? Those students should be brought up on charges, as well as barred from borrowing any other materials until their case is settled."

"Oh, great" groaned David. "I don't need this just when I was about to tackle faculty who allow their reserve book lists to yellow like they do their lecture notes," forgetting that Gustave's reserve books had also been called into question.

"What do you mean?" asked Gustave warily.

"Oh, nothing, nothing," responded David, realizing that he was again about to act first and think later. "Forget I said that. Do you really think that bringing the students up on charges of violating the Honor Code is the appropriate way to handle this problem? Why don't I just call them in and warn them that continued misuse of the reserve system will lead to serious consequences? That should take care of it. I hate for the library to be seen as the enemy after I've worked so hard over the past year to make it a user-friendly place. Barring students from use of library materials prevents their making maximum use of educational opportunities. And word gets around. Let's just handle it informally."

"I don't think so," responded Gustave. "It will mean that they will have gotten away with cheating and not been punished. That's not fair. It's against Orangeville's tradition."

Among Orangeville's norms that David found unpleasant, the Honor Code was perhaps the most annoying. A set of rules of behavior agreed to by students, faculty and administration, the Honor Code was sufficiently ambiguous so that each semester there were intense discussions about what the community considered infractions and what it did not. "I have no quarrel with an Honor Code," David thought. "Its just this never-ceasing debate about what represents inappropriate behavior and what does not that drives me up the wall. And now Gustave wants overdue library books to be included."

\*               \*               \*

How does David solve his twin problems - too many reserves and a request for denial of library privileges?

# CASE TEN

## *THE RIGHT JOB*

"In these times of limited budgets and job freezes, I guess I'm lucky to have not one, but two good colleges - Cooper and Dickens - offering me entry level reference positions," thought Julia Clark. "But how do I decide between them?"

"Both are small schools, one in rural Ohio and the other in rural Indiana, not much difference there. Both are good-looking, have grounds that are well cared for; both have long-standing traditions, although Dickens dates back to the mid-nineteenth century and Cooper to the beginning of the twentieth. They are offering starting salaries that are almost equal and the benefit packages are certainly commensurate."

Taking her yellow-lined notepad, she began to make lists of the two schools' characteristics, noting the factors she considered most salient to the decision at hand.

This is how her lists appeared:

|                        | Cooper    | Dickens   |
|------------------------|-----------|-----------|
| **Student Body**       |           |           |
| Size                   | 1685      | 2065      |
| Average SAT            | 580Q      | 650Q      |
|                        | 540V      | 620V      |
| Place in HS class      |           |           |
| Top Fifth              | 2/5       | 1/5       |
| Percentage             | 82%       | 91%       |
|                        |           |           |
| **Faculty**            |           |           |
| Size                   | 111       | 220       |
| Annual Turnover        | 6%        | 10%       |
|                        |           |           |
| **Administration**     |           |           |
| No. of top Admins.     | 30        | 40        |
| Length in Office       |           |           |
| - President            | 5         | 15        |
| - Provost              | 4         | 16        |
|                        |           |           |
| **Library**            |           |           |
| No. of Volumes         | 260,000   | 480,000   |
| Budget (thousands)     | $950      | $1,600    |
| % for Materials        | 25%       | 40%       |
| No. of Library         |           |           |
| Professionals          | 9         | 6         |
| Length in Office       |           |           |
| - Director             | 5         | 19        |
| Librarian Reports to   | Provost   | Pres.     |
| Status of Library      |           |           |
| Staff                  | Acad.     | Direc.    |
|                        |           | Faculty   |

"These facts tell me something, but certainly not enough to make a decision," thought Julia. "I need to review what I learned during my interviews, and perhaps that will clarify matters."

Cooper sent a Security Department driver to meet me at the airport. From him I gathered that town-gown relations are cordial, that many community residents are graduates of the college and remain loyal alumni. At Dickens I discovered substantially less good feeling between the community and the college. Students are seen by the town as carelessly wealthy, spoiled, unthinking in their behavior.

The Dickens Director picked me up at the plane. He was laid back, courtly, cultured. Asked me what I had concluded about the relative merits of Trollope, Richardson and Austen after completing the research for my undergraduate thesis. He said he, too, had read these authors with great care when he was in school, but assumed that deconstructionist, feminist and other post-modernist criticism had substantially altered the way in which each was currently viewed.

Cooper's Director had asked me to prepare a short talk on my understanding of the nature of college information work, to which he had invited all the other professional library staff. In the question period that followed, he and the others sought my opinions about the new "information literacy" concept, the use of CD-ROM, end-user data base searching, the acceptability of charging fees, and how I viewed the future of libraries. They were a lively and challenging group. After the presentation, the Director delivered me to the President, who had prepared a group

of library "scenarios" to pose to me. He listened intently
to my answers, but the meeting was cut short when a
member of the Board of Trustees phoned and I was
ushered out with a handshake.

The Dickens Director slowly walked me through the
library, pointing with pride to the excellent holdings -
legacies, in part, from deceased faculty - and to the
wonderful rare book and manuscripts collections.
"Students from this insitutition," he announced proudly,
"have become important scholars.   For instance," he
continued, "Cynthia Amos, the Victorian specialist,
Lawrence Lubower, the noted classicist, and Bruce Smith,
who teaches and writes about the nature of justice, are all
graduates of Dickens."

Cooper's Director had arranged for two staff members
to take me to dinner at a local restaurant - without him.  I
discovered from them that they admire him, find him fair,
consider the institution a good place to work.  Everybody
in the administration and at the library, from the President
on down and including the Library Director, is ambitious.
Nobody intends to stay at Cooper; each is looking to make
his or her mark and move on to bigger and better
positions.

Dickens' Director entertained me at his home.   He
gave a small dinner party attended by the chairman of the
English Department and his wife, the Provost and his
wife, and a female historian whose specialty is nineteenth-
century English history.   It was obvious that social
interaction between the Director and this group was
frequent and relaxed, and the conversation flowed easily
between academic and campus subjects.  The next day, the

President came to the Director's office for tea and to meet me. He chatted amiably about the history of the institution and asked if I had any questions.

Both libraries have automated their catalogs and have user-friendly data bases. Coopers' campus is wired; Dickens wiring is in the planning stages. Cooper encourages library staff to participate in professional organizations; Dickens urges professional staff to attain second subject master's and to accomplish bibliographic and other scholarly research.

"I don't seem to be coming to a conclusion," Julia lamented. "Perhaps I've posed the wrong question. A better approach might be which of these institutions will help me achieve *my* goals.

\*  \*  \*

Describe a set of needs that Julia might have that will best be served by Cooper College. Similarly, describe a set of needs that Dickens will meet more readily.

What are the differences between the two schools, as described, that may have an impact on the quality of work life, and on the campus environment?

What further information may be required to help determine the basis of her decision?

# CASE ELEVEN

## *THE OBSOLESCENT EMPLOYEE*

Mary Elizabeth Miller had worked at the reference desk of Waverly College for twenty-seven years. Before that she had attended Waverly College as an undergraduate, done a year's work in Comparative Literature at Columbia and earned an MLS at Case Western Reserve University. Mary considered the job of reference librarian to be uniquely suited to her temperament and her needs. Students and faculty questions provided an intellectual challenge and she felt her work to be of considerable importance. In addition, the academic environment permitted her to pursue her own research, and every year or two she published an article on woven carpets. She was particularly interested in early European, hand-woven Brussels, Wilton and velvet Axminster rugs. Every third year she traveled abroad, usually joining a tour sponsored by one of the universities. In the past decade she had visited Scotland, China and Istanbul. In addition, she had ample time to pursue her greatest passion, flower gardening.

Mary lived with her elderly aunt in a white clapboard house at the edge of the campus. On her return from Case

Western she had contemplated taking her own apartment. But the size of her aunt's house and the garden had provided a powerful incentive to return home. Now, when she walked back and forth from home to the library each day, she applauded that decision, given the scarcity of suitable housing near the college, and the infirmity of her aging relative.

When she accepted the position 27 years ago, Mary had told Jackson Parks, then head librarian, that she would gladly work evenings or weekends at any time. She understood that the rhythm of student life was certainly not attuned to the nine-to-five day that guided most of the work world. Students were as likely, or more so, to have a question at 10 o'clock on a Friday evening as at two in the afternoon on a Wednesday, and she was pleased to be available to answer them. Jackson Parks had, of course, been grateful and did indeed schedule her at times when other staff were reluctant or unable to work.

Students liked Mary, as did faculty, particularly those in the humanities. She was willing, patient, and dogged in her pursuit of a fact or a citation. Generations of Waverly students profited from her efforts, and each June scores of alumni interrupted their festivities to check in with her. Some faculty had even engaged her services to prepare bibliographies for their books, which she had initially helped them to research.

For twenty-two of her twenty-seven years at Waverly, Mary had felt contented and fulfilled. In the last five years, however, the satisfaction had diminished as new realities and exigencies emerged. For one, Jackson Parks had retired five years ago. A bibliophile, he had run the library from the perspective of someone who loved books. The collections were superb. His successor was, in Mary's view, everything Jackson would have considered Philistine. Trained in the latest methods at one of the State library schools, Pamela Scott had put all her eggs in the "information science" basket. Soon plans were on the drawing board for an "integrated library system," which would include an Online Public Access Catalog, an automated circulation system, as well as automating most functions of the acquisitions and technical processes. By the second year of Pamela's "reign," as Mary referred to it, OCLC had come to Waverly College, and by the third year "online data-base searching" had arrived.

Mary's colleagues in the reference department - David, Chris, Jane and Emily - had all attended the Dialog training session in St. Louis, but Mary had conveniently contracted a sore throat, her first in twenty-three years, and could not attend. When they returned, full of excitement at the power of the new technology, she managed to find some bibliographic searching that had to be done in the card catalog.

In the fourth year of Pam's directorship, David, Chris, Jane, and now Steve (Emily had taken an advanced position on the West Coast) were routinely conducting on-line data base searches. Mary continued to help students, although, as she complained to the library secretary one day, the current crop was different than their predecessors. They were not as aggressively motivated to acquire knowledge. They sought out reference services far less often, and seemed to lose interest earlier in the process. "I compared my reference statistics this year with those of five years ago, and I was giving reference service to almost twice the number of students then," she said.

A trip to newly accessible Prague during the summer of 1991 helped to restore some of Mary's feelings of harmony with the world, although the nagging feeling that things were changing too fast followed her even there. The old world grandeur and elegance were still apparent in the historic buildings that remained. But she could sense their tenuousness. The people she met asked her how much she earned, how available cars and apartments were in America, and were impatient with her questions about landmarks and memorials. She used her Baedeker to discover the old places, the old customs, the old values.

Her return to Waverly was met with interest. Colleagues, librarians and faculty alike, were waiting to learn about her trip. Some, Giles Wayland-Smith, for instance, of the political science department, were disappointed to hear that she had lost interest in Vaclev Havel when he became head of the country, and had talked to no one about his government. Others, however, such as Carlin Smolev in architecture, had been thrilled with her descriptions of churches and the ancient parliament building.

The reference staff was anxious to report to Mary what had ensued in her absence. "We bought three CD-ROM bibliographic data bases," said Chris, "and the software is so excellent that students can search for themselves after a short description of subject headings and KWIC approaches."

"Oh, that's nice," commented Mary, quick to cover her ignorance. Chris could have been talking Czech or

Slovak for all she understood.

Gathering up all the mail on her desk, she made her way to the staff room to brew a cup of tea and try to catch up on what had happened on the campus and and the library in her absence. She read without interest Simon Moss's memo on the campus rewiring; with mild interest about the SAT scores of incoming first-year students; with greater interest about the new faculty members, particularly about the replacement of Seth Eaton, the Gothic specialist, by Kazuo Omiki who would, to her distress, teach minority and third- world literature; and finally, with some consternation a summary of the year's statistics for the reference department, showing that requests for all kinds of searches - ready reference, in depth - were up by 17% over the previous year. Near the bottom of the pile was a note from Pamela Scott, welcoming her back and asking that she make an appointment as soon as she had "sorted out her desk."

Mary did as requested, set up a date with Pamela for Friday and busied herself becoming familiar with the new reference books that had arrived during the summer. On Friday, she gathered up her notebook and a freshly sharpened pencil, and knocked on Pamela's open office door.

"Hi, Mary. Do sit down. I'm putting the finishing touches on this letter to accompany our Buehl Foundation grant request to hire a consultant for the automation project. I'll be with you in a minute."

Mary looked around the commodious office Pamela had inherited from Jackson. "It may be the same office," she thought, "but it doesn't look or smell like it did." Jackson's bookshelves had been filled with his personal collections, rare and first editions, books with leather bindings that he kept soft with periodic applications of neat's-foot oil. Pamela's shelves held stacks of periodicals about academic libraries - *College and Research Libraries*, the *Journal of Academic Librarianship*, - books about management and about college libraries. "It's just not the same," she mused.

Mary's reverie was broken by Pamela's voice. "What I had in mind," she was saying "was a series of orientation sessions on the new CD-ROM's so that students can use them without help and you and the rest of the reference staff could be free to answer less routine questions. I chose you to give the sessions because you're good with students. You explain things so clearly and concisely."

"But I don't know how to use the equipment," said Mary, "and, as you know, I was sick when everyone had the computer training."

"This is really easy," said Pamela. "The manufacturers called it 'truly user friendly' and they were not exaggerating. Any first-year student will be able to handle the hardware."

"I'd rather not do it," said Mary. "Why don't you let Chris or Steve? They're awfully skillful with computers."

"It doesn't really have anything to do with computers. You just have to learn to press a few buttons," countered Pamela. "Retrieving information from an automated data base requires the same skills you use when you hunt in a traditional index or an abstract. The only thing it gives you is increased access because you can you link terms in a way that you can't possibly do manually."

Straightening her shoulders, her back arching, Mary told Pamela that there was nothing you could do on a computer that you could not do without it and that coddling students by making it so easy for them denied the importance of the search process and even of a liberal arts education itself. "I am sorry," she informed Pamela, "I simply will not participate in the end of intellectual inquiry as we've have always known it. I will continue to do reference as I have done it for the last twenty-seven years." With that, she rose from her seat and made a rapid, albeit dignified, exit.

Pamela stared at the doorway through which Mary had departed. "I'm not surprised," she thought. "I had anticipated resistance at a minimum, and refusal as the most likely outcome. But now I have to take action. I cannot ignore what has happened, nor can I ignore the fact that fewer students are asking Mary for help, that the help she is supplying puts those students at a disadvantage since their access is severely curtailed by having no opportunity to tap the computer resources, that she is not pulling her weight in the department and that it is unacceptable for her to continue her attitude toward any technological advance. What will she do when we install the online catalog and close the card catalog? I tried to appeal to what she does well, but it just didn't work. If she didn't have that relationship with the alumni and humanities faculty, it would be a lot simpler. I wonder what my next best step is?"

CASE TWELVE

# *ERNEST IS NOT TENURED IN THE ENGLISH DEPARTMENT*

Ernest Clayburn, a Ph.D. from Emory University, had been teaching in the English Department at Remson College in South Carolina for six years. An adequate teacher, though somewhat demanding, he was well-liked outside the classroom by both faculty and students. Serious, but with an acerbic wit, Ernest had helped Ron Craft with his Habitat for Humanity group, had been active in the anti-apartheid movement on campus and raising scholarship funds for South African students, had arranged debates on abortion, had brought exciting speakers to the campus and had served on the faculty library committee.

Myra Baker, Director of the Remsen College Library, first came to know Ernest when they had joined together with History Professor Peter Glass in a project funded by the South Carolina Bates Foundation. Their object was to work with the public schools to produce an oral history of the local civil rights movement in the 1960s. Myra and Ernest had successfully opposed Peter when he attempted to have the students present only the successes of the effort.

Myra's next encounter with Ernest occurred when he served on the library committee, and her respect for him grew. It had been years since a member of the committee had taken an active, constructive interest in the library, had raised questions about activities, made suggestions about innovations and participated knowledgeably in budget discussions. When he left the committee after his three-year term had elapsed, she viewed his departure with regret, although she was pleased and relieved to find that his interest in the library continued undiminished. He remained a frequent visitor to her office.

In their sixth year at Remson, faculty members are considered for tenure. Their credentials are evaluated on the basis of three criteria: teaching, scholarly output, and service to the community. Teaching is weighted most heavily, with the other two items considered much less important.

At the beginning of Ernest's sixth year, he began to bring his dossier up to date. In an effort to document his contribution to the community, he asked Myra to write a recommendation describing his work on the oral history project and on the library committee. In her glowing recommendation she mentioned his willingness to inform himself about library matters and to participate in library committee decisions. She praised his moral integrity in the face of pressure to gild the project, and added a personal note about what a genuinely nice person he was. She forwarded the recommendation to the committee and sent a copy to Ernest, who penned a short note of thanks and told her he would see her soon.

Almost a month elapsed between the time Ernest first asked her for a recommendation and her next chance meeting with him.  She was shocked to find him thin and pale.   His usually clean-shaven face showed signs of bristles and his hair was unkempt.  His bloodshot eyes and the slept-in look of his clothes documented still further his sorry state.

"For heaven's sake, Ernest," Myra questioned, "what is going on? I've seen you looking better."

"I learned last week that my department will not recommend me for tenure.  My chair, iron-fisted Burt Van Apple, has decided that I lack 'collegiality,' that I have made friends with members of the sociology department who are number crunchers and whose approach to scholarship lacks dignity and the influence of the human touch.  He subscribes to Carlyle's great man theory and believes that not only history, but all great literature is biography.  I don't mind that he believes that, even though I think it's an untenable position for a teacher of English, but he has turned everyone against me.  All my friends are looking at me strangely and I know there are lies being inserted in my tenure file."

Shocked, not only at his appearance but at his apparent agitation, Myra tried to reassure Ernest.   "The tenure committee will take into account Burt's intransigence when it reviews your case."

"Not a chance, Myra.  Burt is so powerful on this campus that no one will cross him. He is also terribly narrow-minded.  Once he reaches a decision, he will move

heaven and earth to make it stick. Do you know that in all
the years he's been chairman, until five years ago there
was never a Jew, a Catholic, a Black, an Asian or a
woman in the English department.  Today there is one
Catholic and one woman.   None of the others, yet.
Besides, the tenure committee never overturns the
recommendation of the department. If they turn thumbs
down, so does the committee."

Troubled, Myra made her way back to the Library.
Ernest's observations rang true.  The Tenure Committee
rarely made a decision contrary to the wishes of the
department unless there was a split recommendation or a
weak one.  In this case, there appeared to be unanimity,
although with Burt's bullying it was hard to tell whether
the decision represented a consensus or a fear of
challenging the chairman.

The Library had been plagued by an exhibitionist. It
was a matter of some concern, particularly since he had
seen fit to "moon," among others, a trustee's spouse.
True to form, he had reappeared during Myra's absence,
but, once again, the student who had been the target of his
action could not identify a face.   "Other parts of the
anatomy, perhaps," the female student had commented
wryly, "but I don't think I'd like to try."

In the clamor of the moment, Myra forgot about
Ernest and his plight and turned her attention to
speculating about the best way to stop the exhibitionist or
trap him.

About three weeks later, Myra learned that Ernest had
indeed been denied tenure.  She immediately called his

office and asked him to lunch the next day, an invitation he accepted with surprising alacrity. Myra decided that an off-campus site, away from the possibility of being seen or overheard, would be preferable, and she chose the Confederate Arms, an inn about three miles out of town. Swinging around to Brooks Circle to pick up Ernest, she tried to construct remarks that would offer condolences but not condescension. Her shock at Ernest's appearance made her forget her lines and she hastened to get him into the car.

By now a full beard had replaced the patches that had speckled his cheeks and chin the last time, but it was uneven, scraggly and sadly in need of a clipping. Ernest's frame was thinner than it had been three weeks before and his face wore an expression that was simultaneously bellicose and defeated.

"Why are you bothering with me, Myra?" he asked accusingly. "I can't do anything for you anymore. I tried when I was on the library committee, but you have nothing to gain from having lunch with me."

"Oh, Ernest," Myra responded, "I only wanted to tell you how sorry I am about the tenure decision and to give you a chance to talk if you want to. I thought we were friends."

Somewhat abashed, but obviously full of underlying rage, Ernest said that people on the campus had told him that Myra was certainly not his friend. As a matter of fact. with the exception of his wife, Sidra, he had no friends on the campus.

Myra was able to deflect the conversation and channel it into less controversial paths. Lunch passed with a minimum of anger, although Myra had no opportunity to question Ernest about his future plans or to offer, as she desperately wanted to, any help. When she dropped him back at Hafter Hall, she said she hoped they could get together again. Ernest said that he was to see President Seeley on the following day, and perhaps he'd have some news for her then.

True to form, the exhibitionist had struck once again during lunch hour, but this time Ted Sakonich the security guard had chased him down and he had a left-foot loafer.

"Now how did the Prince find Cinderella?" Myra teased the guard.

Shaking his head, he answered, "It's too hard to go that route - try this shoe on every undergraduate's foot. We'll catch him, eventually. Don't worry."

At four-thirty on Wednesday afternoon, Myra received a call from President Seeley's secretary, Sandy, asking her to come to his office at 10:45 the next morning. "Who else will be there?" Myra asked. "You're it," answered Sandy. "No one else has been scheduled." Myra had been to see the President alone twice before in her five years at the college. The first was when she had been on campus two weeks and the President asked her to have tea in her office, an official and pro forma greeting. The second time was when the Board had asked for a direct report from the Librarian and the President wanted to know in advance what she planned to say.

"Perhaps he's concerned about the exhibitionist," Myra thought. "I'm trying to put a stop to it." A little nervous, and more than a trifle curious, Myra arrived at the President's office by 10:30, expecting to spend fifteen minutes chatting with Sandy, an endeavor that always produced information unavailable from any other source. This time, however, Sandy told the President that Myra had arrived and was directed to send her right in.

"Myra," said President Seeley. "Thank you for coming on such short notice. I won't beat around the bush. I know you are a friend of Ernest Clayburn's and that you have seen what a state he is in since the decision. I, too, am an admirer of his. Unfortunately, I cannot overturn the decision. What I would like to propose to you is to take the position Norman Vance is vacating and give it to Ernest."

"But that's a position for a professional librarian in the reference department," countered Myra, as evenly as she possibly could.

"Yes, but Ernest has a Ph.D. and his knowledge of bibliography in the humanities is outstanding. Even his colleagues in the department commented on that. I told Ernest I would ask you, but not put on any pressure. That's not exactly true. I am asking you, and I hope you will say 'yes.' Ernest is a bright, able person who will get over his temporary setback and serve the college well. Will you do it?"

\*　　　　　　\*　　　　　　\*

Is Ernest right for the library? What are the implications of hiring him? Does a Ph.D. equal an MLS? What are the risks of Myra refusing the President? What are the risks of not refusing him?

CASE THIRTEEN

## *PRESERVE AND PROTECT*

James O'Rourke was a little nervous. Actually he was *more* than a little nervous. Albert College in Stilton and Hobson College in Brompton both had had major thefts of rare books and Judson College was a straight line west from those two places. Not only that; Judson College had by far the best rare book collection in the area, thanks to Roy Hilde, oil man and bibliophile, recently deceased. The responsibility for maintaining the security of rare books and manuscripts at Judson usually meant nothing more than ensuring each evening that everything was put away, the door was locked, and the alarm set.

Now, however, James wanted to be sure that every obstacle was placed between Judson's materials and the thief. Besides, he wanted no blame attached to him for negligence. He knocked on the door of Martin Lifshutz, Director of the Library.

"Mr. Lifshutz," he said. "I think I need some advice."

Martin Lifshutz greeted James with a mixture of

amusement and affection, thinking to himself that James sometimes had more the look of a family retainer than the excellent librarian he knew him to be. Small of stature, with stooping shoulders, and with hands that could often be seen washing each other, James shuffled rather than walked. No, thought Martin, he's not the family retainer. He's Uriah Heep as I think Dickens meant him to look.

"Yes, James," he answered. "What can I tell you?"

"I'm sure you've heard about the robberies at Albert and Hobson," began James.

"Yes, I've been reading about them."

"I'm worried that we may be next on the list. It's summer. The place is filled with genealogists. I'm so busy. Anyone could be the thief and I'd never know. There has even been some talk that it could be a faculty member from a college in nearby Illinois, someone who uses the rare book collection and identifies the valuable materials, and later goes back to steal them. We need to take steps to prevent that from happening here."

"What did you have in mind, James?" Martin asked. "You have a good lock, the burglar alarm works, and I know the care you take putting everything away each night."

"There is a rule on the books," said James, "that all packages and briefcases are to be examined as users leave the library, but circulation has been lax about enforcing it. Could you have Rudy Burke, head of circulation, tell his students that they must now be vigilant and look at every patron's belongings."

"That's a tough assignment for Rudy," responded Martin. "Of course, I'll ask him to do it. We've been losing a lot of books from the general collection lately. Students have discovered how to mask the security tape, and more and more books are leaving without ever having been checked out."

Rudy Burke invited James to talk to his student assistants about the importance of having each briefcase, bookbag or package examined.

"While the general run of college materials is important," James told them, "and I certainly don't want to minimize their value, most can be replaced. The rare books are 'sui generis,' one of a kind, and we will not see their like again if they are stolen."

In the days that followed, James wondered if he had gotten the message across to students. Periodically he planted himself in the library lobby, studying the new book shelf and surreptitiously watching to see whether students were indeed examining packages and briefcases. What he observed were some completely conscientious students, others who were apathetic, and still others so deeply in conversation that they buzzed people out without ever lifting an eye to see who was departing. James also noted one troublesome episode between a student assistant and a faculty member, the latter reluctant to comply with library rules and the former shy about insisting he do so.

"Rudy," James called from down the hall, "can I see you for a moment? Some of your students aren't checking people as they leave the library.  Is there anything we can do about it?  I noticed one in particular - Mark, I think his name is - who just ignores everyone but the person to whom he is speaking."

"A troublemaker, that Mark," agreed Rudy, "and the president of the student council, to boot. Very popular on campus.  I don't assign him to shelve anymore because his productivity ranges from little to none. If he could run his hands like he runs his mouth, he would accomplish the world."

"Why don't you fire him?" James inquired.   "Mr. Lifshutz was clear in his February memo that any student staff members who do poor work or who have bad attitudes should be terminated."

"Martin knows about him," Rudy replied.   "But students play a variety of roles in the library.  They work; but they also serve as conduits.  Mark lets me know, in no uncertain terms, how students feel about the library.  And he is always accurate."

"What if the thief passes by the desk when Mark is there?" asked James.  "Good-bye rare book. Also, Rudy, the faculty don't seem to be as cooperative as they might be.  I saw one give a student a hard time when he was asked to open his briefcase."

"It's true," answered Rudy.   "Faculty consider themselves above suspicion, particularly those who use the library with great frequency.  They think, somehow, that everyone should understand that they would never steal anything.  It's not arrogance as  much as expectation.  In addition, it never occurs to faculty that students can be hesitant about confronting them, that they represent authority."

"Well, what can we do, Rudy?" asked James. "How can we get the students to be more vigilant and the faculty to understand why they must make their packages available to examination?"

*     *     *

What kind of actions can Rudy take to insure that students are impressed with the importance of their role as guard/monitor? How can faculty be reached? Is there a role for Martin Lifshutz in persuading faculty to cooperate? If so, how is it best accomplished? How can Mark be encouraged to provide the kind of leadership to student employees that he provides in student campus politics?

## CASE FOURTEEN

## *FRIENDS AND PEERS*

The professional staff at Philadelphia City College had recently been granted faculty status, with most of the rights and privileges available to teaching faculty. The AAUP bargaining unit now represented them in salary negotiations and handled any grievances they might have. While salaries for library faculty remained dramatically lower than those for their teaching colleagues, and though no librarian had yet received a sabbatical, Joyce Freund, Library Director, believed that if the staff accepted the responsibilities and obligations that came with faculty status, other benefits would in time accrue as well.

Philadelphia City College library staff members admired their director, although few would admit to liking her. Blond, regal, distant, she was a crusader for librarians, but never their personal friend. A workaholic, she spent long hours on her job and on research, expecting no less from her staff. Gaining faculty status had been no small accomplishment. Years of argument had been required, during which she had slowly mobilized faculty and administration support, all the while carefully demonstrating the importance of librarians to the educational program of the college. The victory was sweet, but tenuous. She would suffer no laggards or malingerers on the staff who might put her accomplishment at risk.

Bruce Ketcham had been in the reference department for four years. At Philadelphia faculty promotions come after a minimum of four years in grade, and one could become an Associate Professor without having first received tenure. Joyce appointed a three-person committee to review Bruce's performance and to make a recommendation about whether he should be promoted. Promotion generally implied tenure three years later, and it was considered unseemly to promote someone unless tenure was anticipated. After the Committee submitted its recommendation, Joyce would write one for the library and forward it to the Committee on Reappointment and Promotion.

Popular with peers and students, Bruce was funny, courteous, caring and intelligent. He capitalized on his small stature, making jokes about confronting people by looking them in the knee, and rolling his eyes, Groucho Marx style. Running was Bruce's passion. He had done the Boston and New York Marathons, finishing among the top two hundred in both. He ran before coming to work and sometimes again when he finished for the day. At staff parties he could be counted on to suggest innovative new games, though everyone knew who would win if they were knowledge-based. Bruce had come to librarianship from economics, where he had been "All But Dissertation" (ABD) for more years than the statute of limitations allowed.

The library committee consisted of Barbara Kronman, cataloging, Jim Stefanucci, reference, and Pam Greenberg-Hayes, reference. Joyce called Bruce into her office, informed him of the make-up of the committee and asked him to have a packet of materials ready to submit in one month, by October first. In it he should place any publications he had, recommendations from persons he felt could comment on his work, a self-evaluation and an up-to-date resumé.

On October first Joyce forwarded to the committee the materials Bruce had submitted, and also provided them with a current job description and the performance appraisals Bruce had received every year since he had come to Philadelphia City. She also gave committee members a summary of the criteria to be used for evaluating Bruce. These included:

1. Reference ability
2. Quality of library instruction
3. Student and faculty relations
4. Library committee participation
5. Contributions to the profession
6. College-wide committee participation
7. Perceived growth in the job
8. Ability to do independent work
9. Conscientiousness
10. Collegiality.

The Committee met on October 5th. Each member admitted his or her reluctance to judge Bruce. "It's one thing to be evaluated by a supervisor, but it seems wrong to have to decide about friends," said Pam.

"Let's ask Joyce to make the decision," suggested Jim.

"She won't like it," warned Barbara, "but it's worth a try."

As anticipated, a grim and visibly angry Joyce told the committee that their request was not only unacceptable, but dangerous. "Traditional teaching faculty are responsible for judging their peers. They don't concern themselves with friendship and hurt feelings. Their role is to look at performance and potential, not comedic prowess. If you cannot accept this assignment, you ought to leave academic librarianship. Faculty respect comes with meeting responsibilities, not from carrying a title."

Abashed, the Committee reconvened the next day, deliberated, and issued the following report to Joyce:

The Committee to consider the promotion of Bruce Ketcham to Associate Professor met on Thursday, October 6th at 9:30 AM. The ten points were addressed and conclusions reached about each.


In the matter of *reference ability*, the committee judges Bruce to be 'superior' in his ability to locate answers to questions in which he is interested, while recognizing that periodically he is negligent in helping genealogists and students researching topics that he finds not altogether worthy of attention.

In the matter of *quality of library* instruction, the committee judges Bruce to be 'outstanding' in generating interest and in explaining the process of acquiring and judging information, but only 'fair' in preparation and in subject content of instruction sessions. The committee also finds that he has offered fewer sessions per semester than any other member of the reference department.

In the matter of *relations with faculty and students*, the committee judges Bruce to have established 'excellent' working and personal relations. He has a large following of both students and faculty who seek him out when they come to the library.

In the matter of *library committee participation*, the committee judges Bruce 'satisfactory.' His brainstorming ability and his independent judgment make his contributions to a committee exceptional. The committee also finds, however, that committee participation is limited to meetings; that Bruce is derelict in submitting written or oral reports. An assignment by the committee on library orientation to revise the faculty library handbook was not completed.

In the matter of *contributions to the the profession*, the committee judges Bruce to be 'poor.' When granted research funds to create a bibliography on Running and Health, no publication resulted. He has attended no professional meetings, no workshops, nor availed himself of continuing educational opportunities.

In the matter of *college-wide committee participation*, Bruce has been appointed to represent the library on the Public Events Committee and on the Student Judicial Board, and fulfilled these responsibilities with distinction, according to the Chairs of both committees.

In the matter of *perceived growth in the job*, the committee finds that Bruce has increased his knowledge of reference sources, has become familiar with the college's informal as well as formal structure, and has mastered new technologies.

In the matter of *ability to do independent work*, the committee judges Bruce to be 'satisfactory.' His reference approach and accuracy rate are excellent. During slack times, however, he rarely starts new projects unless they are assigned by the Department Head.

In the matter of *conscientiousness*, the committee judges Bruce as 'poor.' He is often late to work, leaves early, sometimes with unfinished work. Reports are left uncompleted.

In the matter of *collegiality*, the committee judges Bruce as 'excellent.' He is well-liked by the entire staff, considerate, careful of colleague's feelings and a pleasure to work with.

Taking all of the above together, the Committee recommends that Bruce be promoted to Associate Professor.

Respectfully submitted,

Barbara Kronman, Jim Stefanucci,
Pam Greenberg-Hayes

Joyce received the report with resignation, having
calculated in advance its contents. The committee had
approached the job seriously, had assessed with
appropriate consideration each of the points raised, had
judged fairly and accurately in each case, and yet, in spite
of notable weaknesses, had recommended promotion.
"Their inexperience with peer review comes shining
through," Joyce concluded. "They damn with faint praise,
but are unwilling to deny promotion. I suppose it's up to
me, now. Do I reverse their decision? Do they want me
to reverse their decision? How will the library
committee's report look to the college-wide Committee on
Reappointment and Promotion? The decision is a daunting
one."

## CASE FIFTEEN

## *WHO STOPS THE BUCK?*

Bob Brauer opened the letter, hands shaking. He could feel his heart racing as he tried to focus his eyes on the words: "The Bazelton Foundation is pleased to inform you that your grant application for $120,000 to purchase an integrated library system for Delta College has been approved..."

"We got it, we got it," he shouted, as his secretary, Eleanore Smithson, came running in.

"We got the grant?" she asked.

"Yes, indeedy, we sure did," Bob answered, hugging her as he danced her around the office. "Let's see what we have to do now. I have to call the Provost, or should I call the President, or the Director of Development...and of course we have to tell the staff...let's tell them first. See how many of them you can find right now. It shouldn't be too busy out there. After all, it's April 15th and 84 degrees. You can hardly walk on the campus without tripping over some bikinied, sun-tan-lotioned student lying on a blanket or the grass. You'd think

91

they'd've heard of skin cancer by now."

Unable yet to contain his excitement, Bob continued to grin and to march around the office. "I did it. I did it," he thought. "Not only are we going to get that catalog up, but we'll get all the parts as well. Grants bring grants. I know I can find another one to cover any shortfall we might have. And just think what it will do for this school. That antiquated catalog with impossible subject headings, never updated. I'm glad we've done so much of the preliminary work, learning what it all means, getting our procedures in shape."

Eleanore had successfully rounded up virtually every professional staff member - only Marybeth was away at a SOLINET meeting in Atlanta - and most of the support staff, leaving three students to cover desks and tell patrons that someone would be available to help them in a very few minutes.

Bob's smile dispelled the anxiety several employees felt when they had received the unprecedented summons to come to the Director's office at once. "Good news, everybody," he announced. "The Bazelton Foundation has given us $120,000 for our automated system. The money will be here in October and I'd like to be ready to start the project then. By next Monday, I will name a committee to study available integrated systems to see which one will best match our needs."

Spontaneous applause startled Bob, and he looked abashed, but proud. "I've got to call the administration," he announced. "But I wanted to tell you first."

A round of phone calls and congratulatory conversations occupied the remainder of Bob's morning. By noon, he was not only hungry but remembered that he had neglected to call Lila to tell her about the grant. On his way out, he told Eleanore that he might be back a little late; he had to buy his wife a celebratory lunch.

Bob Brauer had been at Delta College for ten months. A graduate of the University of Illinois Library School, he had done his undergraduate work at Rice University and was pleased to be back in Mississippi, the state where he had been born and raised. An under-funded Baptist college, Delta had recently undergone a change in administration. The new President and a new Director of Development had pledged to restore financial stability to the institution while continuing to serve its traditional student body, those from less affluent families who required generous infusions of work-study aid and loans.

Many of Bob's colleagues at Illinois had headed for universities, or for the elite liberal arts institutions of the Northeast and Midwest. But Bob's commitment was to the South and to undergraduate education. His contemporaries had termed him a "a vestige of the sixties who belonged in the Peace Corps or Vista," which Bob considered a compliment. On leaving Illinois, he had taken a job at Freeman in South Carolina for three years, then Bobson, in Georgia, for two, and had come to Delta from there.

Bob had been the new administration's first appointment. In the interview he had been told in fairly clear terms that a major part of his job was to find ways to enhance the library through grants. The first two grant requests he had submitted, both for collection development funds, had been denied. The application to the Bazelton Foundation had been the most ambitious.

Bob announced at the staff meeting the following Monday that the automation committee would consist of the heads of the departments: Lois Richter from cataloging, MeiMei Lu from reference, and Ross Murphy, circulation. "I have asked Rich Fredericks from the computer center and Vice-President Winter to sit in the initial meetings. I will attend the meetings, of course, but will not chair the committee. I have decided to name Lois to that position, given her familiarity with technology. My job, as I see it, is to question, advise, and encourage. I will call the first meeting tomorrow morning at 8:30, and Lois will take over after that."

At the next morning's meeting, Bob suggested a plan of action that would include reviewing the available literature, visiting a few places that had already installed integrated systems, preparing an outline of characteristics the system would require, and writing a Request for Proposal. "Don't neglect the staff as you proceed," Bob warned. "Frequent consultation and orientation help to allay fears and rally support. Don't be afraid to make a decision, but bear in mind that we must live with the final choice for at least five years. Now it's all yours, Lois."

Bob knew he had picked wisely when he put Lois in charge. Watching her guide the group, organize a schedule and make assignments convinced him not only that she was the right choice, but that he was lucky to have her on staff. Gratitude spilled over to Multi-Container Corporation for their having the good sense to hire Lois's husband at an extraordinary salary to manage their Delta plant. That, and the college's child care program for Lois's three-year old son, kept her content to run the catalog department. Bob was aware that she had been offered the Directorship by the previous college administration and had turned it down, not wanting at this time in her life the responsibilities and extra hours that doing the job well would demand.

On October 11, the deadline date that Bob had established for making a decision, the committee scheduled a marathon session to review the five responses to the Request For Proposal that had been submitted. They began at 9:00 AM. Lois had ordered in lunch, warning the food service that dinner might be required, as well.

Bob had attended most of the committee meetings, but had also turned his attention to writing grant requests for a comprehensive bibliographic instruction program which involved meeting with the college's 94 full-time faculty to learn how many were willing to participate and at what level. As a result, he found himself racing through the proposals on the night before the meeting, cramming, he thought, just like an undergraduate. Clearly, from his perspective, the choice boiled down to Techni-Systems and Inte-Pac, with the latter offering better functional modules, but with no history of installed systems, and the former, Techni-Systems, lesser capabilities, but a superb track record.

The meeting began promptly, with Lois distributing a summary of the proposals received, listing their assets and drawbacks, and a list of priorities for the system that had been established at one of the earlier meetings of the committee. She informed the group that Rich Fredericks and Vice-President Winter had been consulted and their recommendations would be shared with the committee after all the proposals had been considered.

By the morning coffee break, two proposals had been discussed; by lunch they had completed four;  by the afternoon break, all had been investigated and comparisons made among them.  By dinner time, the college's and the library's priorities had been applied and the choice narrowed to the two Bob had considered best.   Lois informed the group that Fredericks had opted for Inte-Pac, but that Winter had strongly urged them to choose Techni-Systems because he had more confidence in the company.

So much work accomplished, and yet the difficult decision lies ahead, thought Bob, as he excused himself to call Lila and tell her to have dinner without him.  Winter's recommendation had given Bob pause.  It had really not occurred to him to consider seriously the financial condition of the company.  It seemed to him that any company that could bid at the level the integrated system would cost had to be solid.  But perhaps not.  Had Lois checked the company's financial stability, he wondered. That would be all we would need.  Bankruptcy.  There goes our track record; our ability to attract other grants. It's not my style, but this time we may have to go with safe.

Bob reentered the room, to find Lois summarizing the important features of each system.  Inte-Pac's reserve system was exceptional,as was its acquisitions system. Techni-Systems had full Boolean search capability in its OPAC as well as an elegant circulation system.   The discussion moved to consideration of service.

Inte-Pac had offered to make available a technician for the first three weeks in which the system was to operate. In addition, the committee found company representatives agreeable and easy to work with. Techni-Systems representatives were helpful, but certainly more business-like. "Verging on arrogant, I'd say," commented Ross. They had laughed when the suggestion was made to provide a technician for three weeks and had compromised by agreeing to make someone available on campus for one week following installation, assuring committee members that their well-developed user information office was staffed and could be consulted by phone twenty-four hours a day. Bob asked whether Lois had investigated the financial solvency of Inte-Pac.

"Yes, I did, Bob. This would be their first installation as a company, although their President worked for Apple, the Vice President for LIBRIS and their designer for DEC. They have only been in business for seven months."

Bob listened carefully to comments made by each committee member. Taking their lead from Lois, a tilt toward Inte-Pac was becoming increasingly evident. He could hardly blame them. The company members were engaging and exciting in their vision, their package was innovative and offered features that would provide better service. But that financial uncertainty is probably too risky for us right now.

"Let's break for dinner," Bob suggested, "and when we come back, we'll make the final decision."

During dinner Bob knew, he must decide his own course of action.  "Can I live with the Committee's decision, no matter what it is?  Should I intrude? To what extent should I make my preferences known?  Do I really believe in participatory management?  Can I put my money where my mouth is?  What does it mean to be the library director?"

When Lois asked what he would have for dinner, he replied, distractedly, "Indigestion."

## CASE SIXTEEN

## *AT THE JUDGE'S BEHEST*

Ex-Justice of the New Vermont State Supreme Court Charles Bingham beamed at Michelle Cummings, Director of the Friendship Library at Leister College, from behind his oversized, uncluttered desk in the law offices of Bingham and Bingham. "What can I do for you, Michelle?" he asked.

"But, Judge," she responded, "you sent for me."

"I did, indeed. I had forgotten. I'm so used to people asking me for things. Has President Higgins told you of my intention to take my papers from the State Library and put them here? I thought of the plan last week when I was flying back from New Delhi. Why should the State Library have them when I grew up here, went to Leister, lived here, raised my family here, ran for Judge from here, and served as Interim President of the college when Higgins took a leave of absence to consult with the Ford Foundation in Afghanistan?"

His gnarled finger pointed instructions at her. "Now, little lady," he said, "what I want you to do is go tomorrow

to the State Library, look at the boxes, figure out how to
get them here, and tell me next week what we need to do.
That's a good girl."

Dismissed, Michelle walked out of Bingham's office
in a rage. "Little lady, good girl," she muttered. "How
could I sit there and take it? Little lady! she repeated.
"I've only gained thirty pounds since I took the job.
Nobody could possibly mistake me for a little lady. Good
girl! Forty two years old and I'm a good girl. Why do I
even bother to work in this place? Every time I have to
meet with one of those trustees, I feel like I'm back a
whole century and that they regard me as the one who uses
her feather duster on the shelves, writes catalog cards in
the library hand, and personally checks out each book. If
the library weren't so excellent, the students so exciting,
and the budget so generous, I certainly wouldn't hang
around here."

Making her way up the hill back to the campus,
Michelle mentally reviewed her calendar for the next few
days. It's not a good time, she thought, but I've got to do
it if the President wants me to. Perhaps I'd better call him
to find out just what's going on.

President Higgins differed from his trustees, though
not much. A little younger, a little more exposed to the
prevailing social winds, he had been willing to consider,
for instance, parental leave and a liberalized sabbatical
policy for faculty, although any support he might have
given to them evaporated in the face of trustee opposition.
Higgins had been at Leister College too long - almost 30
years - had become too accustomed to hobnobbing with the
Heads of Standard Steel and Allied Industries. His

greatest pleasure now was his 12:30 martini at the Leister Union Club with Clare Festinger, retired President of KeyDrive Tool Company.

When Michelle entered President Higgins' office at 3:30, she found him, back to the desk, apparently staring out across the campus from the French doors that opened on a landscaped terrace. Clearing her throat, she called softly, so as not to startle him, "President Higgins, it's Michelle Cummings."

Receiving no response, she tiptoed around the desk, only to discover Higgins fast asleep, mouth agape, snoring very quietly. She tapped him on the shoulder, causing his body to shudder and his eyes to fly open.

"Oh, Michelle, I am sorry. I was waiting for you, and my eyes must have closed. Sit down," Higgins suggested, indicating the leather chair in front of his desk. "Now why did you have to see me so quickly?"

"I was summoned to the Judge's office this morning, and told, in no uncertain terms, that I would go to Burlingville tomorrow morning, look at his papers and determine the best way to transport them here for our special collections. I just wanted to check with you before I went."

"Is he going ahead with that hare-brained scheme? I thought I talked him out of it. Well, I guess you better go. You know how the Board admires Charles. Anything he does is okay with them. Let me know what you find."

Michelle decided to take the train to Burlingville. It

would give her time to do some professional reading and she wouldn't have to fight the traffic. I'll take along this Sara Paretsky mystery in case I get tired of the other stuff. Who am I fooling? she asked herself, as she jettisoned *College and Research Libraries* and the *Journal of Academic Librarianship*, leaving only the paperback detective novel in her bag.

The State Library in Burlingville was housed in the State Office Building. Its reference collections and some of its archives were available to the public. But most of the extensive manuscript collections were located underground, occupying close to a half-mile of shelves and bins. The head of the manuscripts collection eyed her strangely as she asked to see Bingham's papers. "They are closed," Rick McCullough, the manuscripts librarian informed Michelle.

"I don't want to see what's in them," she said. "I only have to look at how much space they occupy and what kind of containers they are in."

"It's a big collection," Rick asserted. "One of our biggest. I think he must have kept every laundry list he ever made. C'mon, I'll show it to you. Why do you want to see it?"

"The Judge has decided that he wishes to place the collection at Leister College and I am to survey it and decide how it can best be transported and housed once it arrives there," Michelle responded.

"That's interesting," said Rick. "But I think you have four problems. The first is that we have a signed statement from the Judge giving us permanent possession of the collection. The second is that there is doubt about who owns the public papers, the State or the Judge. The third is that it occupies so much space that you would need a new wing at the very least to house it. And the fourth is an ethical question. Do you think it is appropriate for you to have the collection, considering that you serve only undergraduate students and they don't do the kind of research that these papers could be used for? And that's not even talking about the expense of moving them."

"Listen," said Michelle. "I'd be happy to do without the collection. I don't need it. I don't want it. But I have to deal with the Judge. Have you met him? He's impossible. And I could have serious problems with the library budget if I don't do what he asks me to."

"Here's where the collection starts," Rick pointed to a series of cardboard boxes. "And here's where it ends," he said, about two minutes later. "It's about 300 cubic feet."

Michelle swallowed hard. There was certainly no room in the library for that collection - although it might be a way to get a new addition, she reasoned. On the other hand, we might have to sue the State Library, and who says we'd win? Finally, what good would all those papers do? I can't get into them for fifty years. Would we ever have the money to catalog them? And if we did, who would use them out there in the boondocks of Vermont? On the other hand, who would want to use them, considering the undistinguished career of Charles Bingham? Would the papers have anything of value? Turning them down could have serious ramifications for the College and for the Library. There were other collections owned by other trustees and friends of Charles Bingham that she coveted. Refusing Charles's collection might have a spillover effect on those other collections. Charles was extremely wealthy. It was well known that the bulk of his estate, with the exception of a few bequests to his daughters and other family members, would go to the College. Would a decision not to accept his collection jeopardize the Library's endowment?

Thanking Rick for his assistance, and responding to his question about what she intended to do with an "I don't know" shrug of her shoulders, she caught the 4:30 train out of Burlingville. Try as she might, she could not concentrate on what V.I. Warshowsky was doing to solve the murder, and finally, giving up, she put the book back in her purse. She attempted to think through the problem as she stared out into the gathering darkness. She knew that her first step tomorrow would be to see President Higgins. But what would she tell him?

CASE SEVENTEEN

# *AN IMAGE PROBLEM*


The appointment of Freda Kuby to the Bridgeton State College Curriculum Committee represented a moral victory for the library even though she would serve only ex-officio and would not be a voting member. In the pecking order of committee importance devised by the Ad Hoc Governance Commission, the Curriculum Committee was second only to the Faculty Council, an elected body that acted as sounding board for the President and advised him on matters of tenure and promotion. Larry Koenig, College Librarian, had lobbied hard for a seat on the Curriculum Committee, contending that the library's most important role was to support the curriculum. Since new programs were constantly being suggested, and sometimes established without attention to whether there were sufficient library materials to sustain them, library representation on the Curriculum Committee seemed appropriate.

Freda had come to Bridgeton as Associate Director/Head of Public Services from the University of Minnesota, where she had,worked in General Reference

Services.   She had joined the Bridgeton staff because it
represented a promotion and also because she liked Larry
Koenig.   He was innovative, had good instincts about the
role of library service and believed ultimately in the ability
of libraries to change people's lives.   He, too, was
relatively new at Bridgeton, had started two years before
she had and was making changes gradually, but with
determination.

Quiet,   almost   taciturn,   Freda   was   intelligent,
competent, and commanded deep respect from those with
whom she worked. Reference staff members learned
quickly that the logic guiding her approach to information
retrieval, coupled with her knowledge of current literature
in most fields, made her a court of first resort when they
were stumped by a question. Gradually, too, they came to
appreciate   her   subtle   humor   and   to   overlook   her
self-effacing barbs.

Administrative obligations prevented her from frequent
duty at the Reference Desk, a circumstance she regretted,
secretly fearing that she might, indeed, be a product of the
Peter Principle, having, she thought,  risen to her level of
greatest incompetence;   she   was   also   afraid   that   her
reference skills were withering away from non-use. Back-
office responsibilities kept her relatively isolated from
faculty and students.   Assignment to the Curriculum
Committee was not only a welcome change, but an
opportunity to learn more about the intellectual vitality and
the politics of the college.

Curriculum Committee meetings were held in the
Provost's Meeting Room at 4:10 on Tuesday afternoons.
Membership consisted of two faculty members from each

of Social Sciences, Humanities and Natural Sciences, two students, the Provost, and, ex-officio, the Assistant to the Provost and Freda as representative of the Library. Provost Williams introduced the two students to the faculty members and pulled out his agenda.

"Excuse me, Stan, I don't think I've met the woman sitting on your left," declared courtly Ted George, Chairman of the English Department.

"I'm sorry, Freda, everybody. I thought you all knew each other. This is Freda Kuby from the Library," apologized Provost Williams. "She is going to sit with us, ex officio, as a regular member of the committee, although she will be non-voting."

"I don't think she ought to be here. Who made the decision to include the library? Isn't membership of this committee up to the faculty?" a contentious Mike Barron of the Political Science Department objected.

"I asked Larry Koenig to name someone," responded Provost Williams. "The Curriculum Committee considered the matter at great length last year and voted to invite a library representative to join, ex-officio. It's all there in the minutes."

Mike Barron emitted a walrus-like sound that resembled "Harumph."

"Let's get on with it," said Stan Williams. "The Philosophy Department has forwarded a syllabus for a proposed course in Genetic Ethics to be team-taught by Gabe Waterby and Elizabeth Reddick."

"Shouldn't that be called the Ethics of Genetic Engineering?" asked Tony Hightower of the Mathematics Department.

"They purposely made it more encompassing," replied Stan, "in order to consider such matters as nature versus nurture in the development of intelligence."

"I'll make a motion that we adopt this course as Philosophy 428," Barbara Fisher proposed.

"Second," called Ted George.

"All in favor. Carried," said Stan.

The hour and a half meeting was devoted to approving new courses and dropping old ones. At the close of the session, Stan outlined the work of the Committee for the coming academic year:

"We have to get ready for Middle States. An ad hoc committee will be formed for that purpose and they will give us our assignment. We want to look at the proposal for restructuring the Environmental Science Major to include more public administration and economics courses. The History Department has requested to leave the social sciences division for the Humanities. We need to consider their proposal, although it would destroy the balance among the three divisions. Finally, we have a request from two departments, Psychology and Physics, to review the library. I think we will have one or two meetings devoted to this topic in November.

"Anything else? If not, this meeting is adjourned."

Freda wandered back to the library, musing about the meeting and the interplay of personalities. As was her style in new situations, she had said nothing, only watched. "Serving on the committee will make this an interesting year," she thought, "particularly when they begin to talk about the library."

Larry Koenig listened attentively to Freda's report on the Curriculum Committee meeting.

"Hang in there," he said. "Don't worry about Mike Barron. He was just continuing his battle with the Provost about turf and rights. Stan is an octopus whose tentacles reach out to every corner of this campus. Mike jealously guards what he sees as traditional faculty prerogatives, which he perceives Stan is trying to usurp. He may be right. Stan is nothing if not ambitious, although he has been kind to us so far."

The level of Freda's participation in Curriculum Committee deliberations increased as she grew more familiar with both the members and the issues. She frequently found herself allied with Mike Barron on matters of policy, although her non-voting status saved her from having to side publicly with him against the Provost. She had met Mike one day while walking to the mailroom to pick up a package and was surprised to find him smiling at her, so used had she become to his glaring at the Provost. "Are you enjoying the Committee?" he asked. "Oh, yes," she answered. "And I'm learning a great deal about this institution."

"I bet you are," he asserted. "Listen, I want to ask you something. Why did you come to Bridgeton? You're obviously excellent. Minnesota's a far better school. The students are more able. The faculty is doing interesting research. And the library here is so poor. Everyone says so, all over the campus."

Taken aback, Freda nonetheless answered forthrightly. "You're right. A state college with 8,000 mediocre students and a faculty without scholarly leanings may not be the ideal place to work. But Larry Koenig is doing some of the most exciting, innovative library work in the country today. He will soon replace Blake Giddings of Western as the 'Dean of College Librarians' and I am lucky to have a chance to work with him. He's been here less than three years and already the place has turned around. He went out to recruit me. Came to Minneapolis and offered me the job, although he went through the motions of advertising the position. There were no punches pulled. He told me what an abominable state the library was in and how he took the job for that very reason.

His first priority was to shore up the staff. There was only one position unfilled last year. This year we have a retirement and a resignation. The second front, Larry told me during the interview, is book collections. His predecessor had ordered only what faculty sent her on *Choice* cards, and had weeded any materials in poor condition, without replacing even those which might be seminal in an academic field. Third, fourth and fifth priorities are on the drawing board. He has plans to redo the interior of the library to make it more inviting; to make this a 'wired' campus in a 'smart' building. The staff has been sent to Dialog training to sharpen their online skills. I could go on and on. Tell me, Mike. I hope I don't embarrass you when I ask, when you were last in the library?"

"I am embarrassed," responded Mike, sheepishly. "And I won't tell you. But I'll be there soon."

As the day of the meeting to consider the library neared, Freda sensed an imminent disaster. Perhaps Larry should attend instead of me, or with me, she thought. But when asked, he rejected the notion, observing that she now had a relationship with the committee, and they might be hesitant to speak out in front of him. Arriving at the meeting at 4:05, Freda was surprised to find two non-members Bill Siska of Psychology and Jim Cohen of Physics, already there. Freda dimly remembered that their two departments had been responsible for the request to take up the library, and assumed they had been invited to present their position.

The rest of the members arrived and took their customary seats, and the Provost called the meeting to order.

"It's probably my imagination," thought Freda, "but nobody seems to want to go eyeball to eyeball with me. They don't even want to look at me."

Stan opened the meeting, perfunctorily handling changes in course numbers and other minor matters. "On the agenda today is consideration of the library. I have taken a small, informal survey of the faculty and have come up with the following report. It is confidential, and must be returned to me at the close of the meeting."

Freda read the survey, an outward calm belying her shame and embarrassment. Of the eighty faculty members surveyed, sixty reported unhappiness with the library's holdings. Surprisingly, the remaining twenty claimed that the library was providing excellent reference service and that the collections were far better than they had been in the past ten years. In general, the Humanists regretted the absence of classics in the book collection and the scientists complained of the lack of periodicals. Thirty of the eighty expressed concern about the capability of librarians to provide professional service, several repeating the results of unhappy encounters in years past. The students on the committee had also surveyed their constituents, although their results differed substantially from those reported by Stan. Students commented that the handling of reserves had greatly improved in the last year, that there were more magazines that they liked to read, and that the library's hours were now far more suited to the work schedule of students than they had been. Students continued to complain about the favoritism shown faculty in the length of time that materials could be borrowed.

Silence followed these reports. Freda sat mute, wondering if she should respond or just let the meeting take whatever course it would. She had decided to say at least something in defense of the library, when she heard Mike's voice:

"I would have said the same thing as my colleagues before today, but I just spent an hour and half in the library before coming to this meeting. I have to say the faculty is dead wrong. The library has turned into an exciting place. The reference librarian showed me the Government Documents guide on CD-ROM, and I saw the new video collection. The attitude of the staff has changed. It was an eye-opening experience."

Stan turned to Bill Siska and Jim Cohen. "Your departments asked for this consideration. Do you have a statement?"

Siska of Psychology began. "I have in my hand a list of periodicals we were receiving two years ago," he intoned imperiously, waving a sheath of papers. "This is how many periodicals in psychology the library subscribes to today," he continued, holding up a page. "We are down from 320 to 80."

"You were getting 320 periodicals in psychology?" an incredulous Barbara Fisher asked. "We were getting 35 journals in economics. No matter how much we complained, we could never get any more. But since last year we have been getting 60."

"Jim, did you want to say something for the Physics Department?" Stan asked.

"You may have lost periodicals," Jim told Bill, "but we lost our library. The Physics Department had been building an excellent collection of core materials in the Physics seminar room. Our students never had to go to the library. And if I needed to consult a book or a periodical, I just had to go next door. Now Koenig has called in the library. Told me some story about providing better library service for the whole student body. I don't like it. I want my library back."

The discussion continued long after the usual adjournment time. No action was taken, but Freda was asked to inform Larry about the discussion and to report back the library's responses to the complaints.

Freda wasted no time. She called Larry at home that evening to tell him what had ensued and they agreed to begin the next morning to map a strategy that would inform the committee about the library.

&ast;  &ast;  &ast;

What can you suggest that would help Freda and Larry with their task? Is it possible that Larry has been derelict in some aspects of his job? In what ways?

CASE EIGHTEEN

## *ALUMNI BLUES*

Still sporting the crew cut he had first acquired during his tour in the Navy at the end of World War II, Calvin Webster had the figure and face of a man twenty years younger than his seventy-five years. Clad in sneakers, a tee shirt and wash pants, he had recently installed the library into his daily schedule. It fit somewhere between his two-mile walk and his morning doughnut at the Market House with the Pastor of the Lutheran Church, of whose Board he was President.

An alumnus of Greenfield College, since retiring two years ago Cal had increasingly exhibited a proprietary interest in the institution, and in particular in its Library. At first, he had simply used the periodical reading room, where he had read *The Wall Street Journal*. Gradually he discovered *Barron's*, *Forbes*, and other business periodicals. His reading spilled over into the recreational book shelf and he began borrowing mysteries and current novels. Nobody paid much attention, except to welcome him cordially. As an alumnus, he had unlimited access to the collections.

One day he stopped by to see Library Director Anne Clark in her office.

"Just want to tell you what a fine library you have here," he called from the doorway. "I know how busy you must be so I won't take your time." with that, he disappeared, and Anne, pleased with the praise, went back to contemplating the library's monthly use statistics.

About a week later, Anne looked up to find Cal in her office doorway.

"Can you help me for a minute? I understand that you are fluent in French. Can you read this letter for me?" he asked.

"I'll try," responded Anne, "although my French is rusty. I lived there fifteen years ago, but have scarcely used it since."

"Just read the French aloud, and I can probably understand. My mother was French, and I learned to speak it as child, although I never could read it. She died when I was six and that ended my French training," Cal explained.

Anne began reading, hesitantly at first, fearful that her Southern accent might interfere. True to his contention, however, Cal could indeed understand her words. The few unfamiliar phrases they looked up in a French dictionary. Half an hour later, a grateful Calvin Webster folded the letter back into its envelope, thanked Anne profusely, and left.

On Thursday of the same week, Daniel Roberts, head of Reference Services, came to Anne to ask whether on-line data base searching was part of alumni prerogatives. Cal Webster had asked whether they would do a search on new treatments for Epstein-Barr Syndrome. His neighbor's father-in-law had just contracted the disease and he wanted to know all about it.

"It's easy enough," Anne said. "We can certainly do that for him. Just tap into *Index Medicus* and give him the bibliography."

"But what if he wants the articles after that?" asked Daniel.

"He can go to the medical library at the hospital. They get all those periodicals," Anne instructed.

"Okay," said Daniel. "Thanks for the advice."

The following Monday morning Cal was back at Anne's door. "I would like to answer that French letter. If I dictate, could you write it down for me?" he requested.

"I'm awfully sorry, Cal, I'm on my way out to a meeting. Why don't you go over to the French department. Someone there can probably do a much better job," she told him.

"Good idea," Cal responded, obviously disappointed. "I'll do that."

Anne found herself cooling her heels outside the

Provost's office. "He's running late, today," his secretary, April Westerly, informed her. "The President had some sort of 'in my office on the double' emergency, and that put everything back twenty minutes."

"I'm going down the hall to C. Knights' office," said Anne. "I want to ask him a question. I'll be right back."

C. Knights, Vice President in Charge of Development, was a special friend of Anne's. Two displaced North Carolinians, they could sink into exaggerated down-home drawls when they were alone together.

"So what can I do for you, honey-chile?" C. inquired.

"It ain't nothin C., just a little naggin' feeling that I'm in for a spot of tribulation," she told him.

"Lak what?" he pried.

"Like Calvin Webster," she answered, dropping the game. "Do you know him? How important is he as an alum? As a townie? As a benefactor?"

"Yes. Very. Very. Unknown," responded C. "He is the President of the Alumni Association; he serves on very important committees in this town and is part of the local elite. His *potential* as a benefactor is great. When he retired from Cambridge Carbide, he took with him five million dollars. But as of now, we've seen none of it. He is very tight with his money. His gift to the annual fund has been $100 for the last twelve years and we've been told we're lucky to get that. Cal's wife died fifteen years ago and it was a late marriage at that. They never had any

children.  But there is lots of competition for his money.
Pastor Brickner at the Lutheran Church has doughnuts with
him every morning;   he works at the Red Cross on
Thursday afternoons;    serves on the Board of the
Historical Society and on the Recreational Complex
Authority.  But he has been silent about his intentions.
Why do you ask?"

"He's become a real presence in the Library and I
don't know how far we have to go to keep him friendly,"
Anne told C., and described Cal's recent behavior.

"Everything you can do, you'd better," said C. "And
this college will be eternally grateful.  I hadn't realized
that we had become such an important part of his life.
That's really good."

When Anne returned from the Provost's office, she
was met by a petulant Daniel Roberts. "What's the
matter?" Anne asked her Reference Librarian with more
concern than she felt.   "He can be such a whiner,
sometimes," she thought.

"It's Calvin Webster again,"  Daniel complained.  "I
was trying to learn the two new data bases Dialog has
added this month.  When he saw me at the terminal, he
asked if I would search the SEC Report of Sawyer, Inc.
He's thinking about investing some money and wants to
read about its financial condition.  I tried to explain how
expensive that data-base is, but he interrupted and told me
to come ask you.  I started to object, but something told
me I'd better not."

"Good thinking, Daniel," Anne soothed.  "How long

does the search take?"

"It's a short one. I can do it in ten minutes. But that data base is $200 an hour. It will cost over $30," Daniel answered.

"Then do it. I learned from C. that Cal is potentially a big contributor, and that his treatment in the library may influence his donating behavior. Be nice, you hear?" Anne admonished Daniel as he turned to leave.

Daniel was back two days later. "Now he wants to track the historical Jesus. He's located all sorts of books in theological school libraries that he wants us to borrow for him," he grumbled. "Not only is it time-consuming, but it's not legal according to the interlibrary loan code."

"Oh, Daniel, I know what a pest he has become. Give him to the interlibrary loan people. They'll borrow his books for him. I'm sorry," she told him helplessly.

This is really turning into a problem, thought Anne. But we'll handle it.

The following Monday she arrived at her office at about 9:30, her jaw swollen from novocaine and beginning to ache, as her dentist had warned her it might when he was filling the molar. Calvin Webster sat in her secretary's office, explaining his morning routine to Alane, who nodded politely at appropriate times.

"Oh, Anne," he said. "I've been waiting for you. You look terrible. Perhaps I'd better come back tomorrow. I was going to ask you to help me write a speech about the history of Greenfield, and particularly of the library. I'll be delivering it at the Men's Literary Club on the seventeenth. I bet you know a lot about the subject and could write it real easily."

"I'm not feeling very well, Cal," Anne responded with obvious discomfort." I really can't think today.  Come back tomorrow and we'll talk about it."

       \*     \*     \*

What does Anne tell Cal when he returns on Tuesday morning? Should she, in fact, write his speech? What is the extent of her obligation to him as an alumnus and as a potential donor? What services does the college owe to its non-campus constituencies? If she decides not to write the history, how does she minimize the damage to her, to the Library and to the College?

# CASE NINETEEN

## *THE SINGLE MOM*

Mickey Pastine rushed worriedly into Head of Reference Ben Maloney's office.

"The school just called," she explained breathlessly. "Hilary's sick again and I've got to go pick her up. I'll find someone to watch her and be back as soon as I can."

Not again, thought Ben, his shoulders sagging. That's the third time in two weeks. And it's only Tuesday. I knew we shouldn't have hired her. But Rachel, the Library Director, said that we had no right to discriminate against a single mother and that if Mickey felt she could do the job, we ought to give her the chance.

Ben pulled out Mickey's file, in which he had been documenting her work record, and noted the hours she had missed in recent months. He turned to the front of the file and began reading its contents.

Her application for employment documented her exceptional qualifications. Mickey had come to West Forest from the University of Michigan Library School

122

which she had attended on an American Library Association full scholarship. She had achieved a straight A grade point average. The MLS was her second Master's Degree. Her MA in Literature from Duke University had been earned "with distinction" and a portion of her Master's Thesis had been published in *PMLA*.

Mickey's recommendations were next in the file. "I wish someone would make those comments about me," thought Ben ruefully, as he spied such phrases as "Best student I ever had." "Creative, imaginative, intelligent and thoroughly competent." My last performance evaluation from Rachel read: "Somewhat authoritarian, tends toward rigidity and at home in a bureaucratic environment." Of course she also talked about my leadership strengths and the respect I engendered from the staff, but those may have been afterthoughts.

Ben recalled Mickey's interview for the reference job. Bouncy, she had delighted Rachel with her answers to the questions presented to her. When asked in what reference source she would look when a student requested information on Congressional oversight, she had shrugged her head and rolled her eyes. "Lord knows until I've discovered what the question is about, the dimensions of the problem and what level of information is being sought." All of the other candidates had named specific reference titles - *CQ, The New York Times, SSCI*. Even Ben grudgingly admitted the superiority of her responses. But he had still opposed her appointment. Working mothers with young kids bothered him. He didn't much care that she was a single mother. Only that she had a six-year-old.

Rachel, the Director, a firm believer in participatory management and of joining authority with responsibility, had left the choice to him, but had stressed that discrimination in any form was against library policy. He could select any of the candidates provided he felt that he or she was best qualified for the position. She left him little choice, and Mickey was hired.

A quick study, Mickey had mastered the reference room in two weeks, including all of the intricate details and patterns that had developed over the years. The Ready Reference collection, for instance, was shelved in broad categories that bore no relationship to Dewey or LC classification. But she had learned the new arrangement without difficulty and without suggesting that it functioned less well than those that followed strict classification. Ben noted with wry amusement that undergraduates now sought her out when once they had approached whoever was sitting at the reference desk. Her congeniality, coupled with superior skills, made her a great favorite. She was witty, understanding and, best of all, helped students to put their assignments into perspective.

Not only did the undergraduates respond well to her, but staffers, from student aides to professionals in other departments, came to her with questions. In a conversation over tea one day, she had confessed to Ben that unlike other reference librarians, she had a passion for cataloging. "I think it is the most intellectual part of our field. I'm truly interested in the nature of order. Everyone organizes and I think that there are certain principles of organization that can be identified. If I ever go back for a Ph.D., that's what I'll study. I almost majored in

Anthropology as an undergraduate because of the way they classify things." Needless to say, the cataloguers liked her.

The problems with Hilary made themselves known almost at once. Assigned to work on Thursday evenings, Mickey routinely brought Hilary with her and seated her at one of the reading tables with crayons and paper. For an hour or so, from 6 to 7, Hilary would fastidiously draw designs, periodically running to show them to Mickey. As the evening lengthened, however, Hilary's span of attention diminished, and from 8:30 to 9:00, when Mickey's tour was finished, Hilary sat at Mickey's desk and, more often than not, on her lap.

After the third Thursday evening, Ben took Mickey aside and said that Hilary's presence in the Reference Room was unacceptable and that she would have to make other arrangements. Mickey reddened, started to say that she could hardly afford the day sitter, thought better of it and agreed to find someone to stay with Hilary on Thursday evenings. As an afterthought, Ben said "Of course, that also means Saturdays." Mickey's eyes widened. She began to object but retreated into a muttered, "Of course."

Mickey's performance in her first bibliographic instruction session was gifted. No library "tool" was ever mentioned; nor were any library rules discussed. She spoke only about questions and answers, about parameters of research, about first-hand and secondary sources, about contrasting opinions, and so on. Her philosophy of bibliographic instruction, she told Ben, was influenced by the information literacy movement. She sought, she said, to "empower" students by giving them a basic understanding of how to approach data, information and knowledge. Ben was not only impressed with her success in the classroom, but acknowledged to himself that her method had changed his understanding of library instruction and that he now approached the task from a completely different perspective.

The calls from Hilary's school began late in September. Averaging twice a week, they always resulted in Mickey's dashing off for an hour or two. Hilary was a troubled first-grader. She found it difficult to relate to other children, and often was the target of unkind remarks. A spastic stomach, part nerves, part underdeveloped digestive system, found her almost daily in the nurse's office. Frequently, the health problems resulted in phone calls to Mickey to come pick up Hilary. That, in turn, meant locating a neighbor willing to watch her for the afternoon until Mickey finished work.

Each of these sudden departures necessitated finding a desk replacement for Mickey. Once, the call had come immediately before a bibliographic instruction session. Ben had picked up that one. Some staff were becoming restless and resentful. Jacqueline Arthur, for instance, had marched indignantly into his office, demanding that he dock Mickey's pay. "Why should she get the same salary when she's only here half the time?" she accused. "It's not half the time," said Ben, wearily. And KeiKo had, kindly, suggested that they always schedule two reference librarians at the desk no matter the hour or the flow of traffic, in case Mickey had to go home. But Ben knew they could ill afford to duplicate staff, particularly with the cutbacks looming in the next fiscal year.

It's a dilemma, thought Ben. Her excellence weighs against her unpredictability. Picking up the file, he walked slowly toward Rachel's office to confer with the director.

*       *       *

What does he tell Rachel? Does she have advice for him?

## CASE TWENTY

## *THE ASSISTANT*

"Here, I'll show you how to do it," Lucille told Nate, and proceeded to log onto OCLC. "This means that Des Moines Public owns the title. We can ask them for it first, and then go on to Cedar Rapids Community College if DMP doesn't respond within three days."

Nate was grateful for Lucille's help. As the new interlibrary loan and periodicals librarian, and in his first professional job, Nate Willetts realized he needed a substantial amount of assistance. The job had been vacant for five months and Library Director Paul Donovan had told him that the Department's chief library assistant, Lucille Butler, had substituted while they were hunting for a replacement, and had taken over. "She's done an amazing job," said Paul. "But I'm sure she will be grateful to turn the reins over to you and get rid of all that responsibility."

"Now," Lucille continued, "I'm not going to send for this reprint. That student has asked for three others this month. And this one is too expensive."

"Is that policy?" asked Nate. "What is too expensive?"

"We don't have one that I know about. But I'm not going to let those students take advantage of me. This one would cost about ten dollars."

"What's the article about?"

"Super-conductors or something. This isn't a research college. It's a liberal arts institution. Let him wait until he gets to graduate school before he looks at stuff like this."

Troubled, Nate let the matter drop, but that afternoon hunted through the policy manual and looked up ILL requests. The policy in case of doubt - when the material requested might be too expensive or hard to obtain - was to check with the student and the faculty advisor to learn how important the particular item was to a project or interest.

Nate called Ted Welch, Professor of Chemistry, whom he had met over coffee the day before. "Hi, Ted. Nate Willetts in the library here. I have a question about a student who wants to obtain a reprint of an article through interlibrary loan." Nate explained the nature of the request and then asked Ted how legitimate he thought it was.

"Are you kidding?" said Ted. "He's our best science student. MIT, CAL TECH and Princeton are all after him for graduate school. Give him whatever he wants."

"He's got it," responded Nate.

The next morning, an indignant Lucille confronted Nate, waving an ILL form. "Did you order this? I thought we agreed that we wouldn't put it through. I had put the request in my out box with a note telling the student that we had determined that his request could not be met."

"Yes, I know, Lucille, but I had a talk with Ted Welch and he recommended that we obtain the article. Besides," he added, in an unsuccessful attempt to pacify her, "I needed the practice in ordering. Training isn't enough. You have to experience it yourself."

Nate ignored Lucille's annoyance as they proceded through other departmental routines.

"Damn," thought Nate, "she really is good. Knows everything about the interlibrary loan department, and certainly commands a wealth of information about the school."

The Lake County College Library orientation and training program was administered over a period of a month and included introductory sessions in each department. Nate spent a day learning the automation system and its modules. He was given a password number into the system; trained in how to use campus-wide E-Mail; how to track the number of times a periodical had been requested, and how to master the intricacies of the circulation system.

During his day with Paul Donovan and the business

manager, he was given a lesson in how the budget was put together and how to keep track of his part of it.

Two afternoons on the reference desk helped him to understand the type of questions being asked and something about the nature of the student body.

When he finally returned to his department after completing the training, he felt more at home at Lake County College, and ready to assume his place in the organization.

As the days progressed, however, he realized it would be extremely difficult to sit at the helm of his department since that position was, de facto, already occupied. Lucille rushed to meet every student demand, and to greet every faculty member who found his or her way into the office. The mail stopped at her desk before reaching his, and the few items he got to open were letters from college roommates and old friends.

Lucille was efficient, effective, and had good relationships with the college community.

Nate recognized this. The germ of resentment was beginning to grow larger nonetheless. I'm the professional, he thought. But she's making all the decisions. I'm jealous, I know I am. But there can't be two heads, and I'm doing the clerical work in order to keep busy. On the other hand, should I stop her from doing what she obviously does well? Maybe we don't even need a professional in this department. Maybe library science isn't even a profession and libraries could easily be run by college graduates without library degrees.

Obviously some action was called for. Nate didn't
have a clue about what it should be. He hated to run to
Paul Donovan. Pondering the difficulty of the situation
one day, Nate looked up to find Lucille staring down at
him.

"What's up, Lucille?" Nate asked in a neutral voice
hoping his thoughts were not readable just by looking at
his face.

"The semi-annual Iowa Interlibrary Loan Meeting is
being held in Dubuque in March. I've looked over the
program and I'd really like to go. They're going to
discuss the new code, and the philosophy behind it. I
went to the last session they had and made all sorts of
contacts with interlibrary loan librarians throughout the
state. It's been a great help and I know I could profit
from going."

"Give me time to think about it," said Nate, "and to
check into the travel policy of the library. I'll get back to
you soon."

After she left his office, Nate pulled out the staff
policy manual. All meetings of Iowa consortia could be
attended by one member of each department. "I should go
as head of this department," thought Nate. "But she's
already made the contacts, and she's asked to go. It needs
more thought."

That afternoon, Nate received a called from the
Assistant Director's secretary to ask why they had not yet
received his proposed budget and goals and objectives

statement for the following year. They were due last week. Surely Lucille gave him the forms. Could he please get on it and get them back?

When Nate asked Lucille for the forms, she reported that they had been put in in the inter-office mail that morning and were probably, by now, in the Assistant Director's office.

"But Lucille," said Nate, "how come you didn't give them to me?"

"I didn't want to bother you with that kind of project until you've been here longer," Lucille responded. "Besides, it's just make-work. We simply copy down last year's goals, raise the ante in the objectives by about 10% and do the same thing with the proposed budget."

"All right, Lucille," Nate said with resignation. "The time has come for us to talk about our respective roles in this department."

\*　　\*　　\*

What does Nate tell Lucille?

# SUGGESTED READINGS

The following bibliography is designed to provide a point of departure from which students may begin to research aspects of the problems described in the cases. In each instance, four references in addition to the relevant chapters in *Lyle's Administration of the College Library*, 5th ed., are cited. Needless to say, they only mark a beginning of the search for solutions rather than an end.

## Choosing Sides

Coughlin, Caroline, and Gertzog, Alice. *Lyle's Administration of the College Library*, 5th ed, (Metuchen, NJ: Scarecrow Press, 1992). Chapters 2, 5, 8, 14, 15, 18.

Biggs, Mary. "Sources of Tension and Conflict Between Librarians and Faculty." *Journal of Higher Education* 52 (1981).

Farber, Evan. "Collection Development from a College Perspective: A Response," in *College Librarianship*, ed. by William Miller and D. Stephen Rockwood

(Metuchen, NJ: Scarecrow Press, 1981).

Johnson, Richard. "The College Library Collection," in *Advances in Librarianship*, v.14, ed. by Wesley Simon (Chicago: Academic Press, 1986).

Magrill, Rose Mary, and Corbin, John. Acquisitions Management and Collection Development in Libraries, 2nd ed. (Chicago: American Library Association, 1989).

**The Right Person**

Coughlin, Caroline, and Gertzog, Alice. *Lyle's Administration of the College Library*, 5th ed. (Metuchen, NJ: Scarecrow Press, 1992). Chapters 5, 15, 16.

American Library Association. Office for Library Personnel Resources. *Hiring Library Staff*, Topics in Personnel No. 8. (Chicago: American Library Association, 1986).

Association of College and Research Libraries. "Guidelines and Procedures for the Screening and Appointment of Academic Librarians. *College and Research Library News* 38 (September 1977).

Creth, Sheila, and Duda, Frederika. *Personnel Administration in Libraries*. 2nd ed. (New York: Neal Schuman, 1989).

Glaviano, Cliff, and Lam, R. Errol. "Academic Librarians and Affirmative Action: Approaching Cultural

Diversity in the 1990's," *College and Research Libraries* 51 (November 1990).

**Firebell in the Night**

Coughlin, Caroline, and Gertzog, Alice.    *Lyle's Administration of the College Library*, 5th ed. (Metuchen, N.J.: Scarecrow Press, 1992). Chapters 3, 6, 8, 9, 18, 19.

Engle, Michael O.    "Librarianship as Calling: The Philosophy of College Librarianship." *Journal of Academic Librarianship* 12 (March 1986).

Houser, Lloyd, and Schrader, Alvin.    *The Search for a Scientific Profession* (Metuchen, NJ: Scarecrow Press, 1978).

Morris, John.    *The Library Disaster Preparedness Handbook* (Chicago: American Library Association, 1986).

Myers, Gerald E.    *Insurance Manual for Libraries* (Chicago: American Library Association, 1986).

**Mapplethorpe at McMillan**

Coughlin, Caroline, and Gertzog, Alice. *Lyle's Administration of the College Library*, 5th ed. (Metuchen, NJ: Scarecrow Press, 1992). Chapters 5, 8, 11, 13, 15.

American Library Association. *Intellectual Freedom Manual*, 3rd ed. (Chicago:    American Library

Association, 1989).

Finks, Lee W. "Librarianship Needs a New Code of Ethics." *American Libraries* 22 (January 1991).

Hardesty, Larry, and Kaser, David. *What Do Academic Administrators Think About the Library?* A Final Report to the Council on Library Resources. (Washington, D.C.: Council on Library Resources, April 1990).

Intner, Sheila. *Circulation Policy in Academic, Public and School Libraries* (Westport, CT: Greenwood Press, 1987).

## Six Goes into Five How Many Times?

Coughlin, Caroline, and Gertzog, Alice. *Lyle's Administration of the College Library*, 5th ed. (Metuchen, NJ: Scarecrow Press, 1992). Chapters 4, 6, 16.

Atkinson, Hugh C. "The Impact of New Technology on Library Organization." *Bowker Annual of Library and Book Trade Information*, 29th edition (New York: Bowker, 1984).

Ensor, Pat, and others. "Strategic Planning in an Academic Library." *Library Administration and Management* 2 (June 1988).

Johnson, Peggy. "Matrix Management: An Organizational Alternative for Libraries." *Journal of Academic Librarianship* 16 (September 1990).

McCabe, Gerard. "New Patterns for Managing the Small Staff," in *The Smaller Academic Library*, ed. Gerard McCabe (Westport, CT: Greenwood Press, 1988).

**The Tower of Knowledge**

Coughlin, Caroline, and Gertzog, Alice. *Lyle's Administration of the College Library*, 5th ed. (Metuchen, NJ: Scarecrow Press, 1992). Chapters 4, 5, 8, 15, 19.

Boss, Richard. *Information Technologies and Space Planning for Libraries* (Boston: G.K. Hall, 1987).

Holt, Raymond. *Planning Library Buildings and Facilities* (Metuchen, NJ: Scarecrow Press, 1989).

Metcalf, Keyes. *Planning Academic and Research Library Buildings,*, 2nd ed., by Philip Leighton and David Weber (Chicago: American Library Association, 1986).

Smith, Lester E., ed. *Planning Library Buildings: From Decision to Design* (Chicago: American Library Association, 1986).

**Equal Opportunity for Students with Unequal Pocketbooks**

Coughlin, Caroline, and Gertzog, Alice. *Lyle's Administration of the College Library*, 5th ed. (Metuchen, NJ: Scarecrow Press, 1992). Chapters 5, 13, 15, 18.

Boucher, Virginia. *Interlibrary Loan Practices Handbook* (Chicago: American Library Association, 1984).

Intner, Sheila. *Circulation Policy in Academic, Public and School Libraries* (Westport, CT: Greenwood Press, 1987).

Martin, Murray. *Budgetary Controls in Academic Libraries* (Greenwood, CT:JAI Press, 1978).

Prentice, Ann. *Financial Planning for Libraries* (Metuchen, NJ: Scarecrow Press, 1983).

**The Spouse on the Staff**

Coughlin, Caroline, and Gertzog, Alice. *Lyle's Administration of the College Library*, 5th ed. (Metuchen, NJ: Scarecrow Press, 1992). Chapters 4, 5, 9, 14, 15.

Association of College and Research Libraries. *Standards for Ethical Conduct for Rare Books, Manuscripts and Special Collections in Libraries* (Chicago: American Library Association, 1987).

Ford, Vikki. "PR: The State of Public Relations in Academic Libraries." *College and Research Libraries* 46 (September 1985).

Mortimer, R. "Manuscript and Rare Books in an Undergraduate Library." *Wilson Library Bulletin* 58 (October 1983).

Oberg, Larry, and others. "Faculty Perceptions of Librarians at Albion College: Status, Role, Contribution and Contacts." *College and Research Libraries* 50 (March 1989).

**The Honor Code and the Reserve Book Room**

Coughlin, Caroline, and Gertzog, Alice. *Lyle's Administration of the College Library*, 5th ed. (Metuchen, NJ: Scarecrow Press, 1992). Chapters 4, 5, 13, 14, 15.

Breivik, Patricia Senn, and Gee, E. Gordon. *Information Literacy* (New York: American Council on Education, Macmillan, 1989).

Intner, Sheila. *Circulation Policy in Academic, Public and School Libraries* (Westport, CT: Greenwood Press, 1987).

McCabe, Gerard. *The Smaller Academic Library* (Westport, CT: Greenwood Press, 1988).

Milligan, Stuart. "Database of Scanned Reserve Readings." *Electronic Communication in Public Access Systems Forum* (March 14, 1991).

**The Right Job**

Coughlin, Caroline, and Gertzog, Alice. *Lyle's Administration of the College Library*, 5th ed. (Metuchen, NJ: Scarecrow Press, 1992). Chapters 2, 3, 4, 6, 15, 16.

Boyer, Ernest. *College: the Undergraduate Experience in America* (New York: Harper and Row, 1987).

Clark, Burton. *The Distinctive College* (Chicago: Aldine, 1970).

Moran, Barbara. "Career Patterns of Academic Library Administrators," in *Building on the First Century: Proceedings of the Fifth National Conference of the Association of College and Research Libraries*, ed. Jan Fennell. (Chicago: American Library Association, 1989).

Shiflett, Orvin Lee. *Origins of American Academic Librarianship* (Norwood, NJ: Ablex, 1981).

**The Obsolescent Employee**

Coughlin, Caroline, and Gertzog, Alice. *Lyle's Administration of the College Library*, 5th ed. (Metuchen, NJ: Scarecrow Press, 1992). Chapters 7, 12, 15, 16.

American Library Association, Office for Library Personnel Resources. *Managing Employee Performance*. Topics in Personnel, # 11 (Chicago: American Library Association, 1988).

Fox, Elaine. "Employer Checklist for Determining Just Cause Discharge." *Library Personnel News* 4 (Spring 1990).

Jenkins, Barbara Williams. *Performance Appraisal in Academic Libraries* CLIP Note #12 (Chicago:

Association of College and Research Libraries, 1990).

White, Herbert S. *Library Personnel Management* (White Plains, NY: Knowledge Industry Publications, 1985).

**Ernest Is Not Tenured in the English Department**

Coughlin, Caroline, and Gertzog, Alice. *Lyle's Administration of the College Library*, 5th ed. (Metuchen, NJ: Scarecrow Press, 1992). Chapters 3, 5, 6, 15, 16.

American Library Association, Office for Library Personnel Resources. *Hiring Library Staff.* Topics in Personnel, #8 (Chicago: American Library Association, 1986).

Association of College and Research Libraries. "Standards for College Libraries." *College and Research Libraries News* 47 (March 1986).

Houser, Lloyd, and Schrader, Alvin. *The Search for a Scientific Profession* (Metuchen, NJ: Scarecrow Press, 1978).

Lester, June. "Education for Librarianship, A Report Card." *American Libraries* 21 (June 1990).

**Preserve and Protect**

Coughlin, Caroline, and Gertzog, Alice. *Lyle's Administration of the College Library*, 5th ed. (Metuchen, NJ: Scarecrow Press, 1992). Chapters 5, 9, 13, 17.

Brand, Marvina, ed. *Security for Libraries* (Chicago: American Library Association, 1984).

Katham, Michael D., and Katham, Jane McGurn. *Managing Student Workers in College Libraries*. CLIP Note #7 (Chicago: Association of College and Research Libraries, 1986).

Mortimer, R. "Manuscript and Rare Books in an Undergraduate Library." *Wilson Library Bulletin* 58 (October 1983).

Ungarelli, Donald. "Are Our Libraries Safe from Losses?" *Library and Archival Security* 10 (1990).

**Friends and Peers**

Coughlin, Caroline, and Gertzog, Alice. *Lyle's Administration of the College Library*, 5th ed. (Metuchen, NJ: Scarecrow Press, 1992). Chapters 5, 15, 16.

Association of College and Research Libraries. "Guidelines for Academic Status for College and University Libraries," *College and Research Libraries News* 51 (March 1990).

Hardesty, Larry, and Kaser, David. *What Do Academic Administrators Think About the Library?* A Final Report to the Council on Library Resources (Washington, D.C.: April 1990).

Marchant, Maurice. *Participative Management in*

*Academic Libraries* (Westport, CT: Greenwood Press, 1976).

Werrell, Emily, and Sullivan, Laura. "Faculty Status for Academic Libraries: A Review of the Literature." *College and Research Libraries* 48 (March 1987).

**Who Stops the Buck?**

Coughlin, Caroline, and Gertzog, Alice. *Lyle's Administration of the College Library,* 5th ed. (Metuchen, NJ: Scarecrow Press, 1992). Chapters 6, 7, 15, 16, 17, 18.

CAUSE AND EDUCOM. "Evaluation Guidelines for Institutional Information Technology Resources." *EDUCOM Bulletin* 23 (Winter 1988).

Corbin, John. *Managing the Library Automation Project* (Phoenix, AZ: Oryx Press, 1985).

Darling, John R., and Cluff, E. Dale. "Social Style and the Art of Managing Up." *Journal of Academic Librarianship* 12 (January 1987).

Matthews, Joseph, ed. *A Reader on Choosing an Automated Library System* (Chicago: American Library Association, 1983).

**At the Judge's Behest**

Coughlin, Caroline, and Gertzog, Alice. *Lyle's Administration of the College Library*, 5th ed. (Metuchen, NJ: Scarecrow Press, 1992). Chapters 5,

9, 15, 18.

Association of College and Research Libraries. "Standards for Ethical Conduct for Rare Books, Manuscripts and Special Collections in Libraries." *College and Research Libraries News* 48 (March 1987).

Association of College and Research Libraries. *Collection Development Policies for College Libraries*. Clip Note #11. Theresa Taborsky and P. Lenkowski, comps. (Chicago: American Library Association, 1989).

Prentice, Ann. *Finanacial Planning for Libraries* (Metuchen, NJ: Scarecrow Press, 1983).

Wortman, William. *Collection Management* (Chicago: American Library Association, 1989).

**An Image Problem**

Coughlin, Caroline, and Gertzog, Alice. *Lyle's Administration of the College Library*, 5th ed. (Metuchen, NJ: Scarecrow Press, 1992). Chapters 5, 14, 15.

Biggs, Mary. "Sources of Tension and Conflict Between Librarians and Faculty." *Journal of Higher Education* 152 (1981).

Breivik, Patricia Senn, and Gee, E. Gordon. *Information Literacy: Revolution in the Library* (New York: American Council on Education, Macmillan, 1989).

Ford, Vikki. "PR: The State of Public Relations in Academic Libraries." *College and Research Libraries* 46 (September 1985).

Hardesty, Larry, and Kaser, David. *What Do Academic Administrators Think About the Library?* A Final Report to the Council on Library Resources (Washington, D.C.: April 1990).

**Alumni Blues**

Coughlin, Caroline, and Gertzog, Alice. *Lyle's Administration of the College Library,* 5th ed. (Metuchen, NJ: Scarecrow Press, 1992). Chapters 4, 5, 14, 15, 18.

Albritton, Rosie L., and Shaughnessy Thomas. *Developing Leadership Skills: A Sourcebook for Librarians* (Englewood, CO: Libraries Unlimited, 1990).

Association of College and Research Libraries. *Friends of College Libraries.* Clip Note #9. Ronelle Thompson, comp. (Chicago: ACRL, 1987).

Association of College and Research Libraries. *Mission Statements for College Libraries.* Clip Note #5. Larry Hardesty and others, comp. (Chicago: ACRL, 1985).

McCabe, Gerard, ed. *The Smaller Academic Library* (Westport, CT: Greenwood Press, 1988).

## The Single Mom

Coughlin, Caroline, and Gertzog, Alice. *Lyle's Administration of the College Library*, 5th ed. (Metuchen, NJ: Scarecrow Press, 1992). Chapters 15, 16.

American Library Association, Office for Library Personnel Resources. *Managing Employee Performance* Topics in Personnel #11 (Chicago: American Library Association, 1988).

Association of College and Research Libraries. *Performance Appraisal in Academic Libraries*. Clip Note #12 (Chicago: Association of College and Research Libraries, 1990).

Fox, Elaine. "Employer Checklist for Determining Just Cause Discharge." *Library Personnel News* 4 (Spring 1990).

Glaviano, Cliff, and Lam, R. Errol. "Academic Librarians and Affirmative Action: Approaching Cultural Diversity in the 1990's." *College and Research Libraries* 51 (November 1990).

## The Assistant

Coughlin, Caroline, and Gertzog, Alice. *Lyle's Administration of the College Library*, 5th ed. (Metuchen, NJ: Scarecrow Press, 1992). Chapters 3, 13, 16.

American Library Association, Office for Library

Personnel Resources. *Writing Library Job Descriptions*. Topics in Personnel #7 (Chicago: American Library Association, 1984).

Boyer, Laura, and Theimer, William, Jr. "The Use and Training of Nonprofessional Personnel." *College and Research Libraries* 50 (July 1989).

Oberg, Larry. "Paraprofessionals: Shaping the New Reality." Guest Editorial. *College and Research Libraries* 52 (January 1991).

Wilson, Pauline. *Stereotype and Status: Librarians in the United States* (Westport, CT: Greenwood Press, 1984).

# SUBJECT INDEX

# ABOUT THE AUTHOR

ALICE GERTZOG is a graduate of Antioch College. She earned her MLS from Catholic University of Washington and Ph.D. from Rutgers University. Dr. Gertzog has been a librarian at the University of North Carolina, Yale University, and New Haven College. In addition, she has worked in special and public libraries, has been a library consultant, and has taught at the Rutgers University School of Communication, Information, and Library Studies.